THE MAN IN THE IRON MASK

ALEXANDRE DUMAS

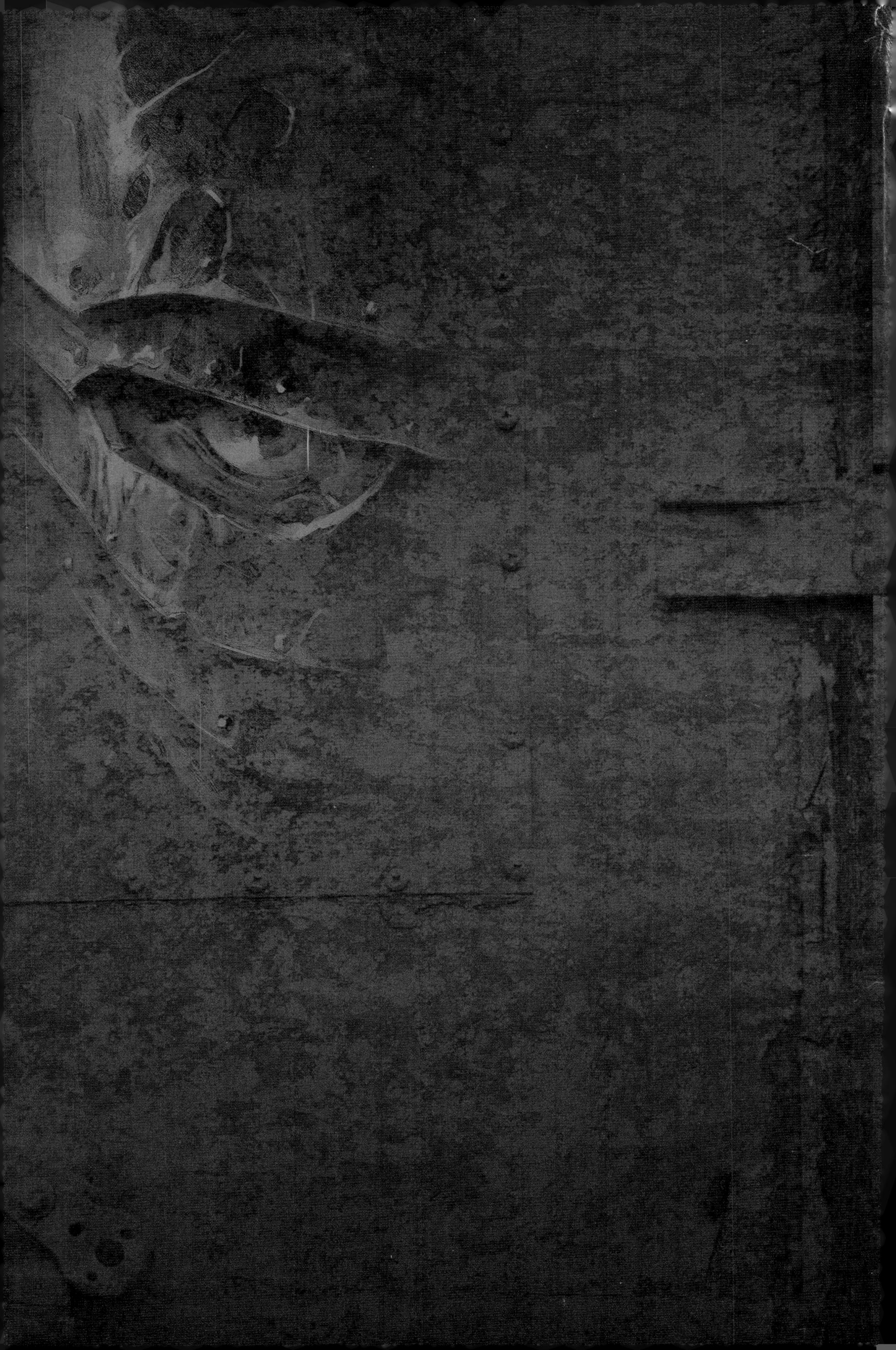

AL GN DUM

THE MAN IN THE
IRON MASK

ALEXANDRE DUMAS

WRITER: **Roy Thomas**

PENCILER: **Hugo Petrus**

INKER: **Tom Palmer**

COLORIST: **June Chung**

LETTERER: **VC's Joe Caramagna**

COVER ARTIST: **Marko Djurdjevic**

ASSISTANT EDITOR: **Lauren Sankovitch**

ASSOCIATE EDITOR: **Nicole Boose**

EDITOR: **Ralph Macchio**

SPECIAL THANKS TO DEBORAH SHERER,
FREEMAN HENRY, CHRIS ALLO & POND SCUM

COLLECTION EDITOR: **Mark D. Beazley**

ASSISTANT EDITORS: **John Denning & Cory Levine**

EDITOR, SPECIAL PROJECTS: **Jennifer Grünwald**

SENIOR EDITOR, SPECIAL PROJECTS: **Jeff Youngquist**

SENIOR VICE PRESIDENT OF SALES: **David Gabriel**

BOOK DESIGNER: **Dave Barry & Dayle Chesler**

VICE PRESIDENT OF CREATIVE: **Tom Marvelli**

EDITOR IN CHIEF: **Joe Quesada**

PUBLISHER: **Dan Buckley**

MARVEL ILLUSTRATED: THE MAN IN THE IRON MASK. Contains material originally published in magazine form as MARVEL ILLUSTRATED: THE MAN IN THE IRON MASK #1-6. First printing 2008. ISBN# 978-0-7851-2592-1. Published by MARVEL PUBLISHING, INC., a subsidiary of MARVEL ENTERTAINMENT, INC. OFFICE OF PUBLICATION: 417 5th Avenue, New York, NY 10016. Copyright © 2007 and 2008 Marvel Characters, Inc. All rights reserved. $19.99 per copy in the U.S. and $32.00 in Canada (GST #R127032852); Canadian Agreement #40668537. All characters featured in this issue and the distinctive names and likenesses thereof, and all related indicia are trademarks of Marvel Characters, Inc. No similarity between any of the names, characters, persons, and/or institutions in this magazine with those of any living or dead person or institution is intended, and any such similarity which may exist is purely coincidental. **Printed in the U.S.A.** ALAN FINE, CEO Marvel Toys & Publishing Divisions and CMO Marvel Entertainment, Inc.; DAVID GABRIEL, SVP of Publishing Sales & Circulation; DAVID BOGART, SVP of Business Affairs & Talent Management; MICHAEL PASCIULLO, VP of Merchandising & Communications; JIM O'KEEFE, VP of Operations & Logistics; DAN CARR, Executive Director of Publishing Technology; JUSTIN F. GABRIE, Director of Editorial Operations; SUSAN CRESPI, Production Manager; STAN LEE, Chairman Emeritus. For information regarding advertising in Marvel Comics or on Marvel.com, please contact Mitch Dane, Advertising Director, at mdane@marvel.com. For Marvel subscription inquiries, please call 800-217-9158.

10 9 8 7 6 5 4 3 2 1

The Man in the Iron Mask:
A Personal Introduction
by Roy Thomas

Of the first three classic works of literature adapted into graphic novel form for the *Marvel Illustrated* series—*The Last of the Mohicans, Treasure Island,* and *The Man in the Iron Mask*—it was Alexandre Dumas' novel, written in the middle of the 19th century, that posed the greatest challenge to this writer.

The first of the so-called "problems" is that, as other notes in this book may likewise relate, *The Man in the Iron Mask* isn't technically a novel at all—but, more accurately, only *one-third* of a truly humongous book whose title is translated into English as *The Viscount of Bragelonne; or, Ten Years Later.* The latter work was so huge and sprawling, in fact, that it was printed in three separate volumes between 1848 and 1850.

What's more, modern-day publishers don't even agree on exactly where the latter portion of *Bragelonne,* which is usually published as *The Man in the Iron Mask,* begins! Some versions start with the scene in which Aramis goes to the Bastille in order to meet the prisoner Philippe and inform him of his true identity, which he has never known. Other renditions, however, commence a bit earlier and include the sequence in which Athos confronts Louis XIV about the king's romance with the woman loved by his son Raoul, the Viscount of Bragelonne—which winds up with Athos nearly being tossed into the Bastille himself.

After due consideration and discussion, editor Ralph Macchio and I chose to have it both ways. The actual *Marvel Illustrated* adaptation of *Iron Mask* begins with Aramis' being shown to the Bastille's cells... while Athos' altercation with France's Sun King is related in two pages preceding that event.

But *why* did we add a several-page Prologue before the action of the novel begins in earnest? It's because of the second of the "problems" related to adapting the story.

For *Bragelonne/Iron Mask* is actually the third novel Dumas wrote about his immortally famed heroes, the Three Musketeers—who, as everyone knows, were really *four* in number, with the younger d'Artagnan as more central to the tale than even Athos, Aramis, and Porthos.

The series began in 1843-44, of course, with *The Three Musketeers*—and was continued by the author in *Twenty Years After* (1845), which picked up that particular "fantastic four" two decades following the episodes told in the earlier book. Ralph and I felt it a good idea to recap, very briefly, the events of the two earlier masterpieces... because virtually everyone who originally read *Bragelonne/Iron Mask* would have been familiar with those previous adventures. These were the same four towering figures of literature—only they were some thirty years older than they'd been when d'Artagnan first came to Paris, fresh off the Gascony farm, in the opening pages of *The Three Musketeers.* The quartet were no longer the young swashbucklers they had been... and, in fact, only d'Artagnan was still a Musketeer at all.

In a sense, we were adapting the trio of tales backward... beginning with the novel in which the ultimate fates of three of the foursome would be revealed. But, if *The Man in the Iron Mask* was indeed a work of art—and it certainly is—it could surely stand on its own, without the necessity of one's reading the earlier books first!

As for the final main "problem" in adapting this novel—it was the Man in the Iron Mask himself!

It was both fitting and ironic that Marvel would adapt this novel... for, after all, when in 1962 they had created the greatest villain in the Marvel Universe, Dr. Victor Von Doom, writer/editor Stan Lee and artist Jack Kirby had clearly been inspired by the image of Dumas' mysterious metal-helmeted figure (who, in turn, was inspired by a very real personage in French history). It's even common knowledge that Darth Vader, that ultimate baddie of George Lucas' *Star Wars* double-trilogy, the first episode of which was adapted as a Marvel comic in 1977, was in turn influenced by Dr. Doom.

The problem: although the Man in the Iron Mask is a powerful, iconic image, he doesn't really appear onstage much in Dumas' novel. Philippe, the tragic twin brother of Louis XIV, dons the iron headpiece by royal command only after he's sent back to the Bastille by the king, after Aramis' scheme to substitute him for the true monarch is exposed. And that is where most adaptations of the novel, whether in film or in the graphic arts or in truncated "young people's" retellings, end. In actual fact, however, Dumas later relates two very dramatic scenes to which the masked Philippe is central… and we were bound and determined to include them in our version.

The Man in the Iron Mask—as part of the longer *Viscount of Bragelonne*—carries the lives of the four once-Musketeers forward for some years… and ends with all of them except Aramis having died at what was, in the 17th century, a reasonably ripe old age. Aramis, the ultimate schemer and Machiavellian manipulator, survives, even thrives. And, while he is old enough at book's end for us to be certain he will shuffle off this mortal coil before too many more years have passed, it is left to the reader's imagination whether he will fall from favor and be disgraced a second time… or will die in bed, celebrated as one of France's great diplomats.

Relating the later lives and deaths of first Porthos, then Athos, and finally even valiant d'Artagnan, completes the epic cycle of Dumas' trilogy of masterworks, and I personally found that far more satisfying than ending on the melodramatic aftermath of a failed plot involving a high-born pawn, with Aramis and Porthos merely riding off into exile.

Thus, in the final analysis, the very "problems" of adapting *The Man in the Iron Mask* into graphic novel form are what made it, we think, worth the doing.

Dumas' classic was, and is, more than simply another exciting chapter in an epic tale whose events spanned perhaps well over decades. It is the apex, the colorful coda, of one of the towering epics of French—and world—literature.

It was a pleasure to adapt it in concert with the thrilling and moody penciling of Hugo Petrus—and to be teamed again with inker Tom Palmer, with whom I labored some years past on well-remembered tales of *Dr. Strange, The X-Men, The Avengers, Conan the Barbarian,* and others.

We're all pleased and proud to have brought a *third* iron-masked icon into the pages of Marvel Comics—and ultimately into this visually stunning graphic novel.

Roy Thomas

Roy Thomas started his career in comics as a writer and editor working with Stan Lee in the early days of the Marvel Age of Comics, where he scripted key runs in The X-Men, The Avengers, Fantastic Four, Daredevil, Amazing Spider-Man, Thor, Sub-Mariner, Dr. Strange, *and others. During the 1970s he wrote the first ten years of Marvel's* Conan the Barbarian *and* Savage Sword of Conan *and launched such series as* The Invaders, The Defenders, Warlock, Iron Fist, *and the revived* X-Men. *In the 1980s he developed* All-Star Squadron, Infinity Inc., *et al., for DC, and co-scripted the sword-and-sorcery films* Fire and Ice *and* Conan the Destroyer. *Over the years he has won numerous awards, including the Alley, Shazam, Eagle, Alfred, and Eisner. Roy and his wife Dann currently live in rural South Carolina, amid a mirthful menagerie of birds and beasts.*

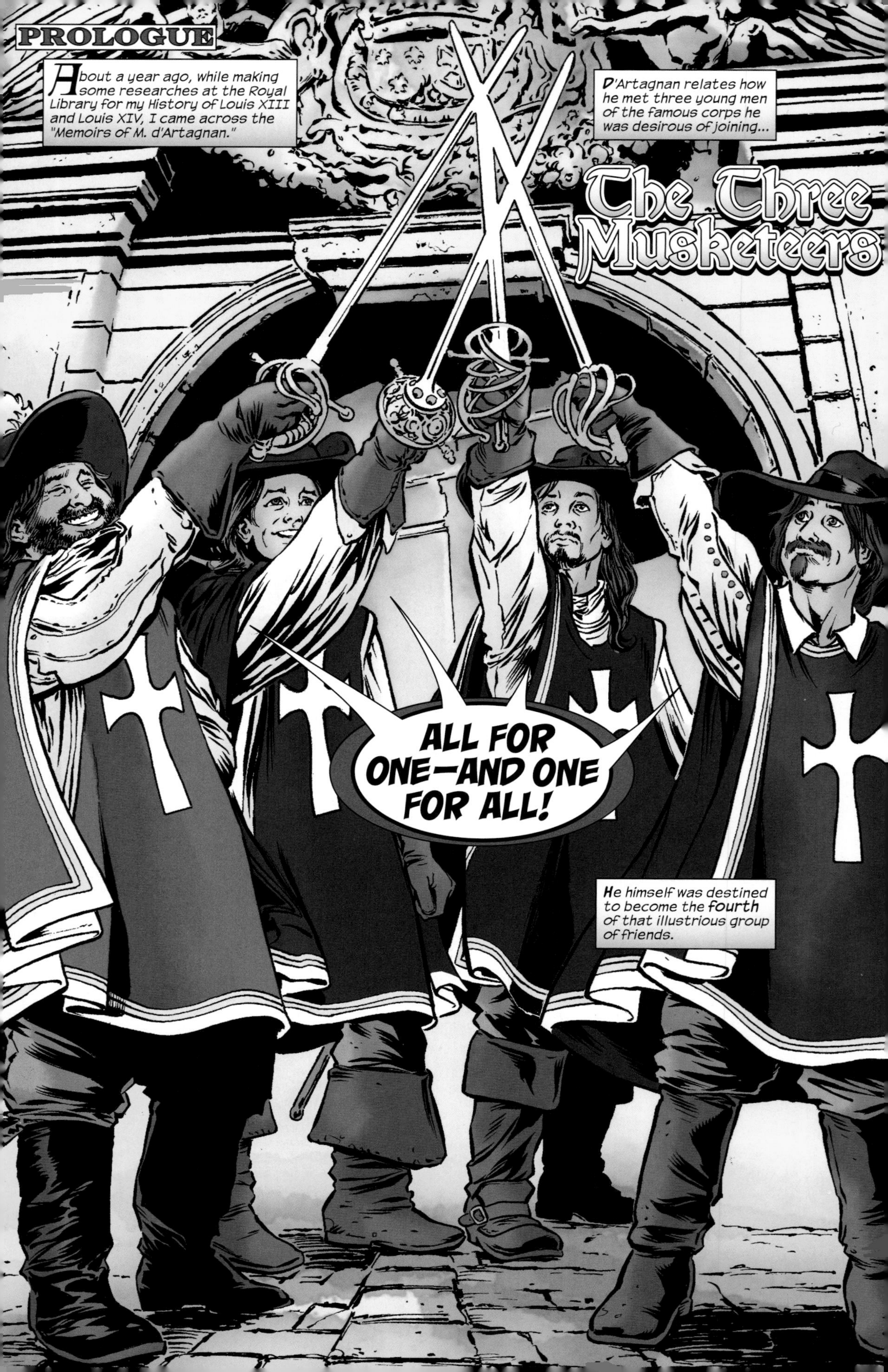
PROLOGUE
About a year ago, while making some researches at the Royal Library for my History of Louis XIII and Louis XIV, I came across the "Memoirs of M. d'Artagnan."
D'Artagnan relates how he met three young men of the famous corps he was desirous of joining...
The Three Musketeers
ALL FOR ONE—AND ONE FOR ALL!
He himself was destined to become the fourth of that illustrious group of friends.

On the first Monday in April 1625, a young Gascon named d'Artagnan arrived in Paris, eager to become a Musketeer...

...and ready to take every smile for an insult, and every look as a provocation.

For he had borne, from his father, a letter of introduction to the Captain of the King's Musketeers...

...and it had been stolen from him on the road.

He was explaining to the captain at his boisterous hotel residence when he spied, outside, the man who took his letter.

He was racing heedless down the stairs...

...when he struck the shoulder of a Musketeer.

OWWWW! You have rudely irritated a recent sword-wound, young man.

It is not **you** who can give me a lesson in good manners, I warn you.

If I were not running after someone...

Mister Gentleman-in-a-Hurry...you can find **Athos** without running after him...

...near the Carnes Deschaux, about noon.

Having thus drawn himself into a duel with a well-respected Musketeer, d'Artagnan again set off running as if the devil possessed him...

...hoping he might yet overtake the thief.

But as he raced between two men talking, the wind blew out the giant one's cape...

Vertubleu! You must be mad!

You must be chastised for running against *Porthos* in this fashion--

--at one o'clock, behind the Luxembourg Garden.

Ahead, d'Artagnan recognized *Aramis* talking to three of the King's guards...

...and resolved to be polite to this third of the trio of famed Musketeers.

I believe, Monsieur Aramis...

...that you stand upon...

...a handkerchief you would be sorry to lose?

You are deceived, sir. This handkerchief is not mine.

But-- I saw--

HAH HAH!

Will you persist in saying, most discreet Aramis, that you are not on good terms with Madame de Bois-Tracy--

--when that gracious lady has the kindness to lend you her handkerchief?

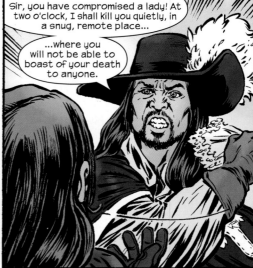

Sir, you have compromised a lady! At two o'clock, I shall kill you quietly, in a snug, remote place...

...where you will not be able to boast of your death to anyone.

Duels at twelve...and one...and two...with three men, each of whom is capable of killing three d'Artagnans.

At least, if I am killed, I shall be killed by a Musketeer!

Being acquainted with no one in Paris, d'Artagnan went to his appointment with Athos without a second...but Athos had *two* such...

I, humble d'Artagnan, offer you my excuses, gentlemen...

...for, M. Athos has the right to kill me first...which will rob M. Porthos and M. Aramis of that pleasure.

En garde!

Par Dieu! This is a clever fellow!

Fighting here, are you, Musketeers--in the shadow of the monastery, in defiance of the edicts?

It was five of the Guards who served Cardinal Richelieu...the Churchman who rivaled in power even Louis XIII himself.

If the King had *his* Musketeers, the Cardinal must have his Guards... and the swordsmen were rivals, even as their masters were.

Gentlemen... sheathe your swords, and follow me--or we will charge upon you!

There are five of them... and we are but three. Yet...

Gentlemen... it appears to me we are *four.*

Well, then! Athos, Porthos, Aramis, and d'Artagnan--

Forward!

And the nine combatants rushed upon each other with a fury that did not exclude a certain degree of method.

Soon, one of the Cardinal's Guards was dead...the others were wounded and fled.

And d'Artagnan's heart swam in delight to be at least an *apprentice* Musketeer.

Later, after a mission involving the Queen, the Duke of Buckingham, and the woman known as "Milady," d'Artagnan was finally offered a commission in the Musketeers.

In time, Athos returned to his estate... Porthos wed a rich widow...Aramis became a monk...and d'Artagnan, a famous soldier.

Twenty years after...

...the four friends united once more, to undertake a mission vital to France.

Their foe on that occasion was the son of "Milady"--he who wore the face of Evil.

More years passed.

By the time the young Louis XIV became King, only d'Artagnan remained a Musketeer, now Captain of the force he once dreamed of joining.

Athos had a noble son...the Viscount Bragelonne, whose name was...

Raoul...

You must cease torturing yourself.

How could I, father...

...when I must watch from a distance as the *woman I love*--the beautiful Louise de la Vallière--has become the mistress of our new young King?

He stole her affections...while I was on a mission for the crown!

I shall speak with the King...for he knows I have wished to contract marriage between yourself and the lady.

But the audience between King and aristocrat did not go well...

Do you hesitate to grant my request, sire?

I do not hesitate. I *refuse.*

I *love* Louise de la Vallière.

Then Athos drew his sword...and broke it across his knee.

Son of Louis XIII, you begin your reign badly--by abduction and disloyalty!

You are now become our enemy, sire.

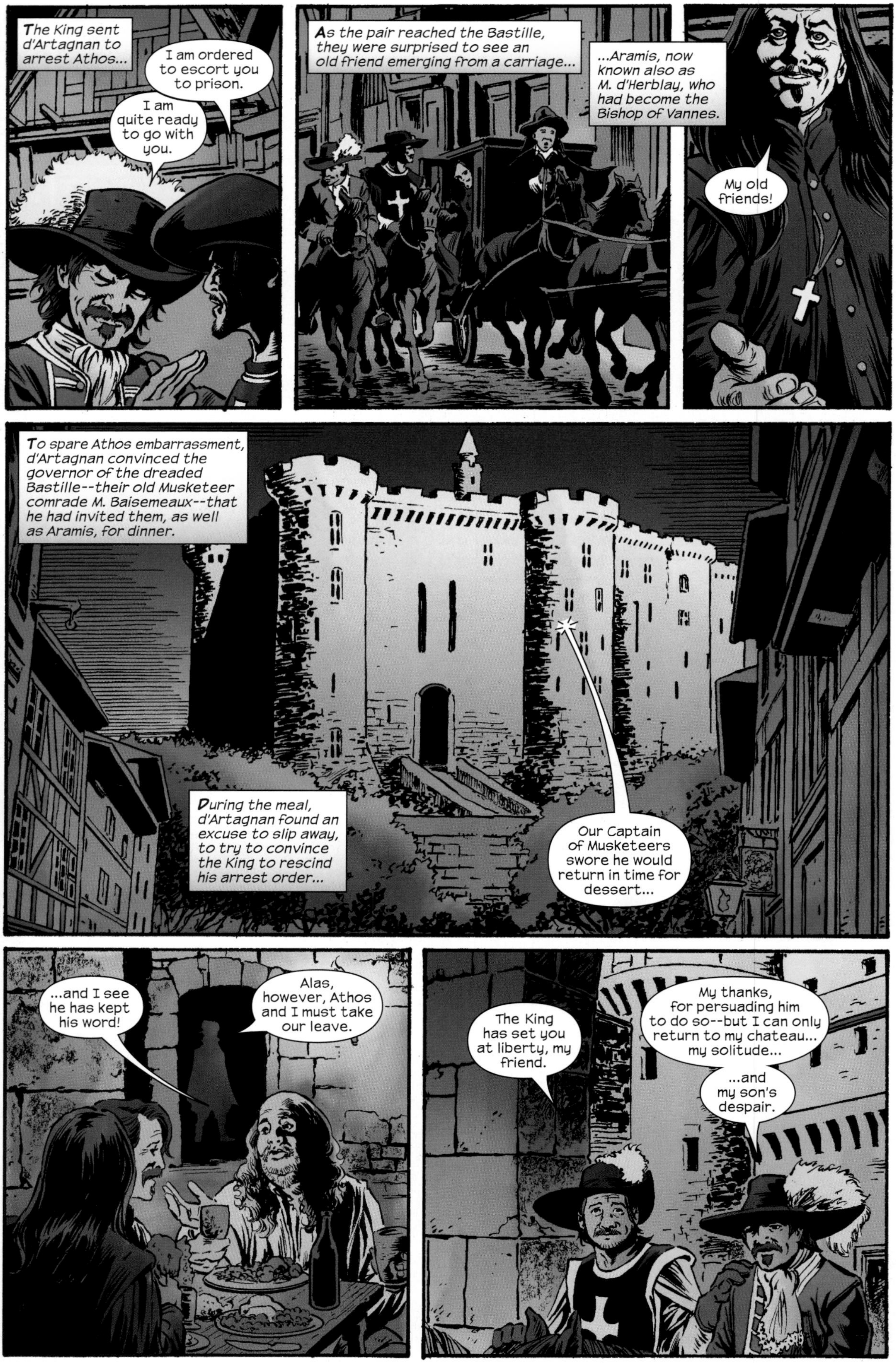
The King sent d'Artagnan to arrest Athos...
I am ordered to escort you to prison.
I am quite ready to go with you.
As the pair reached the Bastille, they were surprised to see an old friend emerging from a carriage...
...Aramis, now known also as M. d'Herblay, who had become the Bishop of Vannes.
My old friends!
To spare Athos embarrassment, d'Artagnan convinced the governor of the dreaded Bastille--their old Musketeer comrade M. Baisemeaux--that he had invited them, as well as Aramis, for dinner.
During the meal, d'Artagnan found an excuse to slip away, to try to convince the King to rescind his arrest order...
Our Captain of Musketeers swore he would return in time for dessert...
...and I see he has kept his word!
Alas, however, Athos and I must take our leave.
The King has set you at liberty, my friend.
My thanks, for persuading him to do so--but I can only return to my chateau... my solitude...
...and my son's despair.

That same night, in the bowels of the dreaded Bastille, there began the affair of...

THE MAN IN THE IRON MASK

The steps of the three men--Baisemeaux, the prison's turnkey, and Aramis--resounded as they reached the basement.

The clinking of the jailer's keys made itself heard, as if to remind the prisoners that liberty was out of their reach.

"No. 12" is ill, and has requested a confessor.

Since you "order" it, M. de Baisemeaux.

But the rules do not allow the governor to hear the prisoner's confession.

I shall wait here, monseigneur.

Why are you here?

Have you not desired a confessor?

Yes.

I thank you for coming.

But I am better...

...and thus I have no longer need of a confessor.

I have seen you before.

Perhaps. And you have nothing, then, to regret?

No.

Not even your liberty?

What do you call liberty, monsieur?

I call liberty the flowers, the air, light, the stars...

...the happiness of going whithersoever the nervous limbs of twenty years of age may wish to carry you.

If flowers constitute liberty, then I am free...

For, I have two roses, gathered yesterday evening from the governor's garden.

With every opening petal, they fill my chamber with a fragrance that embraces it.

When I stand on my chair, the air caresses my face through the bars of my window.

For light, I have the sun, a friend who visits me every day.

As to the stars...I could see them before you entered with your candle.

To return to our starting point...I am your confessor.

First tell me what *crime* I have committed...for, as my conscience does not accuse me, I aver that I am not a criminal.

We are often criminals in the sight of the great of the earth, not for having ourselves committed crimes...

...but because we know that crimes have been committed.

Yes...it is very possible that, in that light, I am a criminal.

And so you desired a confessor...

...after the note you found in your bread bade you ask for one.

If the King were to know of my presence here, I would tomorrow see glitter the executioner's axe...

...or the bottom of a dungeon more gloomy and more obscure than yours.

Since, then, we both wear masks, either let us both retain them... or put them aside together.

Tell me what you remember of your infancy...your childhood.

Perhaps it was then that your crime was committed.

First, I have a right to know--who *are* you?

Do you remember seeing, fifteen or eighteen years ago, in the village of Noisy-le-Sec, where your early years were spent...

"...a cavalier, accompanied by a lady in black silk, with flame-colored ribbons in her hair?"

"Yes. They told me he was the Abbé d'Herblay... who was also one of Louis XIII's Musketeers."

"Well, that Musketeer and Abbé, afterwards Bishop of Vannes, is your confessor now."

"I knew it. I recognized you."

"I was then called Philippe, and lived in a house and garden surrounded with walls whose boundaries I never left...

"...attended only by my tutor and my nurse, Perronnette.

"They were kind to me, but used to tell me that my father and mother were dead.

"Then, one day, eight years ago, I heard him cry out to her...

What is the matter?

The *letter!* A chance puff of air carried it from my desk--and it disappeared down the well--

--our last letter from the *Queen!*

You know she burns her letters every time she comes.

She will never believe that it was lost in this manner--and Mazarin will--

Well, 'tis no use hesitating...

Somebody must go down in the well and retrieve it--

--some villager who cannot read!

Yes! I will obtain a ladder long enough to reach down--

--while you find some stout-hearted youth.

"As soon as they were gone, I ran to the well.

"Something white and luminous glistened in the ripples of the water.

"The well seemed to draw me in with its large mouth and icy breath.

"Scarcely knowing what I was about, I slid down the rope into the abyss.

"I seized the dear letter...

"...which, alas, came in two in my grasp.

"I managed to retrieve the other half, as well, while becoming drenched...

"The writing was already fading, but I read enough to see that my tutor and Perronnette were far more than mere servants...

"...and that I must myself be high-born, since the Queen, Anne of Austria, and Mazarin, the Prime Minister, had commended me to their care.

"I hid, while a local workman found nothing in the well...

"...and my tutor and nurse became even more upset...

"..until they perceived that its brink was all watery.

"My garments were moist...and I was seized with a violent fever.

"I related the whole adventure to them... so that they found the two pieces of the Queen's letter.

"Doubtless the unfortunate lady and gentleman, not daring to keep the occurrence secret, wrote all to the Queen, and sent back to her the torn letter."

Soon afterward, I was arrested and moved to the Bastille...

...and my two attendants disappeared.

What became of them?

They are dead.

Poisoned.

My enemy must have been very cruel, or hard beset by necessity, to assassinate these two innocent people.

In your family, monseigneur... necessity is stern.

Listen...and, in a few words, I will tell what has passed in France since the probable time of your birth.

The late King, Henry XIII, was long anxious about having an heir...

And on the 5th of September, 1638, his Queen, Anne of Austria, gave birth...

"...to a son.

"You are about to hear an account which few could now give...for it refers to a secret thought buried with the dead and entombed in the abyss of the confessional.

"The Queen lay in her room attended by her midwife...

"...whose name was Dame Perronnette...

"...soon, near at hand, the King showed the new-born to the nobility...

"...and all rejoiced.

"Suddenly, unbeknownst to them, the Queen was again taken ill...

"...and the midwife quietly returned to her.

"Soon, Dame Perronnette whispered to the King what had happened.

"He had a *second* son!

"The King's joy had turned to terror.

"As he and Mazarin knew, there is ground for doubting whether the twin who first makes his appearance is the elder by the laws of Heaven and nature.

"One day, the second son might dispute the first's claim to seniority...sowing discord...

"...and engendering *civil war!*

"That very night, the tutor and midwife spirited the second infant away in a carriage to a certain remote place...

"And today, only his mother remains alive to remember that he ever existed."

Monseigneur--in the house you inhabited for your first fifteen years, there were neither looking-glasses nor mirrors?

I have never heard those two words before.

Then--here is a portrait of King Louis XIV, who at this moment reigns upon the throne of France.

And here is a mirror.

It is the same face!

I think that I am lost! The King will never set me free.

But-- *which* of the two *is* the King?

The one the miniature portrays-- or the glass reflects?

The King is he who is on the throne... who is *not* in prison...and who can cause others to be entombed here.

If you desire it, the King will be he who, quitting this dungeon, shall maintain himself upon the throne...upon which his friends shall place him.

I wish you to be King... for the good of humanity.

But-- what would then become of Louis?

If I restore you to your place on your brother's throne, he shall take yours in prison.

But I shall only do so...if you really want to be free...and to be King.

I...would be both.

Then I shall see you one more time only...on the day you leave these gloomy walls...

...my King.

*M*oments later, the Bishop of Vannes left the Bastille...where the secret which overwhelmed him seemed to double the weight of the walls.

*T*he Bishop's carriage conveyed him to Vaux-le-Vicomte, the magnificent estate of M. Nicholas Fouquet, Surintendant-- that is to say, primary tax collector--of all France.

*T*here, preparations were underway for a great fête which was to be held, in honor of Louis XIV...

*B*ut Aramis found Surintendant Fouquet in no very happy mood...

Why do you sigh, monseigneur?

The fête I suggested you give for the King is approaching.

And money is departing.

You promised me millions...

And you shall have them, the day after the King's entrée into Vaux.

My enemy, M. Colbert--the finance minister--poisons my sovereign's mind against me.

He is trying to convince Louis that I have stolen tax money to build this vast estate, which is greater than the King's.

Frankly, Bishop--I fear imprisonment!

Fear not...all will be well.

Meanwhile, I am back to Paris...when you shall have given me a certain letter of cachet.

A poor lad named Marchiali has been in the Bastille these ten years, for two Latin verses he made against the Jesuits.

And he has committed no other crime?

Beyond this, upon my honor, he is as innocent as you or I. So swears his poor, destitute mother.

Oh! Heaven! You sometimes bear with such injustice on earth--

--that I understand why there are wretches who doubt your existence.

The letter--and ten thousand francs for his mother.

Go! And I hope that God will bless those who are mindful of His poor!

So also do I hope.

That night, as Aramis once again dined with M. de Baisemeaux at the Bastille...

Monseigneur...

Eh? Oh, yes...the *courier* who had arrived.

You must wait till we have finished--

Oh, let us see what he has brought you, old friend...

This message is quite urgent, sire.

It is the business of ministers to write and torment me when I am at rest, and to trouble me when I am happy.

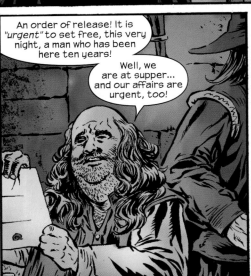

An order of release! It is *"urgent"* to set free, this very night, a man who has been here ten years!

Well, we are at supper... and our affairs are urgent, too!

Dear Baisemeaux, I am a priest...and charity has higher claims upon me than hunger and thirst.

I entreat you, please release the poor devil at once.

Because *you* desire it...I shall summon my servant François.

François, tell the major to go and open the cell of M. Seldon, No. 3, Bertaudière.

"Seldon"? Surely you meant to say *"Marchiali."*

No...the letter said *"Seldon,"* in large letters.

And I read "*Marchiali*" in even larger letters.

Yes--*yes*! Marchiali! 'Tis plainly written Marchiali!

The man of whom we have talked so much?

The very same prisoner whom, the other day...

...a priest, a confessor of our order, came to visit?

It is sometimes good, M. Baisemeaux, that the man of today should no longer know what the man of yesterday did.

But, to relieve your mind... I shall write a note approving the release of Marchiali.

Half an hour later, whilst Aramis watched from out of sight, Philippe was made acquainted with the order which set him at liberty...

You must swear never to reveal anything that you have seen or heard in the Bastille.

I swear with my lips on this crucifix.

Now you are free, monsieur...whither do you intend going?

I--I do not--

I am here to render the gentleman whatever service he may please to ask.

God have you in his holy keeping!

Good night to you, M. Baisemeaux.

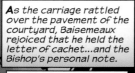

As the carriage rattled over the pavement of the courtyard, Baisemeaux rejoiced that he held the letter of cachet...and the Bishop's personal note.

If any questioned his actions this night, they would prove that he did only that which was commanded of him by his superiors.

After tomorrow, you will sit upon the throne, from which the will of Heaven will have hurled your brother, without hope of return.

His blood will not be shed?

You will be sole arbiter of his fate.

I cannot take my brother's wife.

I will persuade Spain to consent to a divorce.

The imprisoned King will speak!

Aye--to the walls!

Monseigneur--I offer you a secluded estate, where you may let the years of your life roll away, if you have not the heart for our enterprise.

The choice is yours.

Before I determine, let me walk...and consult that still voice within me.

Driver! Halt the carriage!

Ten minutes is all I ask... and then you shall have your answer.

The ineffable whisper of liberty spoke to the Prince in so seducing a language that he could not restrain his emotion...and breathed a sigh of joy.

He inhaled the perfumed air...

...as it was wafted in gentle gusts across his uplifted face.

Then he returned to the carriage... and to Aramis.

Let us go where the crown of France is to be found!

You have perused all the notes I sent, to acquaint you with those who compose your court?

I know them by heart.

My mother, Anne of Austria, and all her sorrows.

Colbert, the minister of finance...

Your friend d'Artagnan... captain of the Musketeers.

The Comte de la Fère... the former Athos...

...and M. du Vallon... Porthos.

And what do you wish for yourself, Bishop?

Merely to be made, in due time, a Cardinal, monseigneur.

And, in due time, as I have given you the throne of France...

...you will confer on me the throne of St. Peter.

With what we may do together, not even Charlemagne will be able to reach to half your stature.

When you shall point out to me the necessary steps to be taken to secure your election as Pope...

...I will take them.

And they resumed their places in the carriage...

...which sped rapidly along the road leading to Vaux-le-Vicomte.

15 August...the day preceding the fête given by Monsieur Fouquet:

Within his royal carriage, the youthful King was most eager for amusements... and thus very desirous to arrive at Vaux-le-Vicomte as early as possible.

For only twice during the journey had he been able to catch a glimpse of his beloved, Louise de la Vallière...

...and he suspected that his only opportunity of speaking to her might be after nightfall, in the gardens of the château.

Thus, he had left most of his enormous entourage behind at Mêlun, and would arrive at Vaux relatively unescorted.

"We go to see a friend as friends," the King had declared.

D'Artagnan, captain of the Musketeers, had encouraged his sovereign in this action...

...saying that M. Fouquet, the master of Vaux, was a man of honor.

All the same, certain questions welled up within d'Artagnan.

Why had his old friend Aramis, now Bishop of Vannes, been so interested recently in seeing the King's new costumes for the fête?

And why, of late, had he become so mixed up in the affairs of Surintendant Fouquet, collector of taxes?

He had no doubt that Aramis had some motive in that...

...and he resolved to address himself directly to his erstwhile Musketeer comrade, when next they met.

What could Aramis' object possibly be-- unless it were to overthrow Fouquet's rival, M. Colbert?

Within the carriage bearing the Queen and the Queen-Mother, King Louis frowned, recalling an earlier conversation with his finance minister, M. Colbert...

Surely Your Majesty will sleep here in Mêlun, and proceed to Vaux in the morning.

What? When M. Fouquet is expecting us this evening?

You other gentlemen may go slowly... but we will ride on.

Louis had known that Colbert merely wished to cause annoyance to M. Fouquet, who was anxiously awaiting the royal party's arrival.

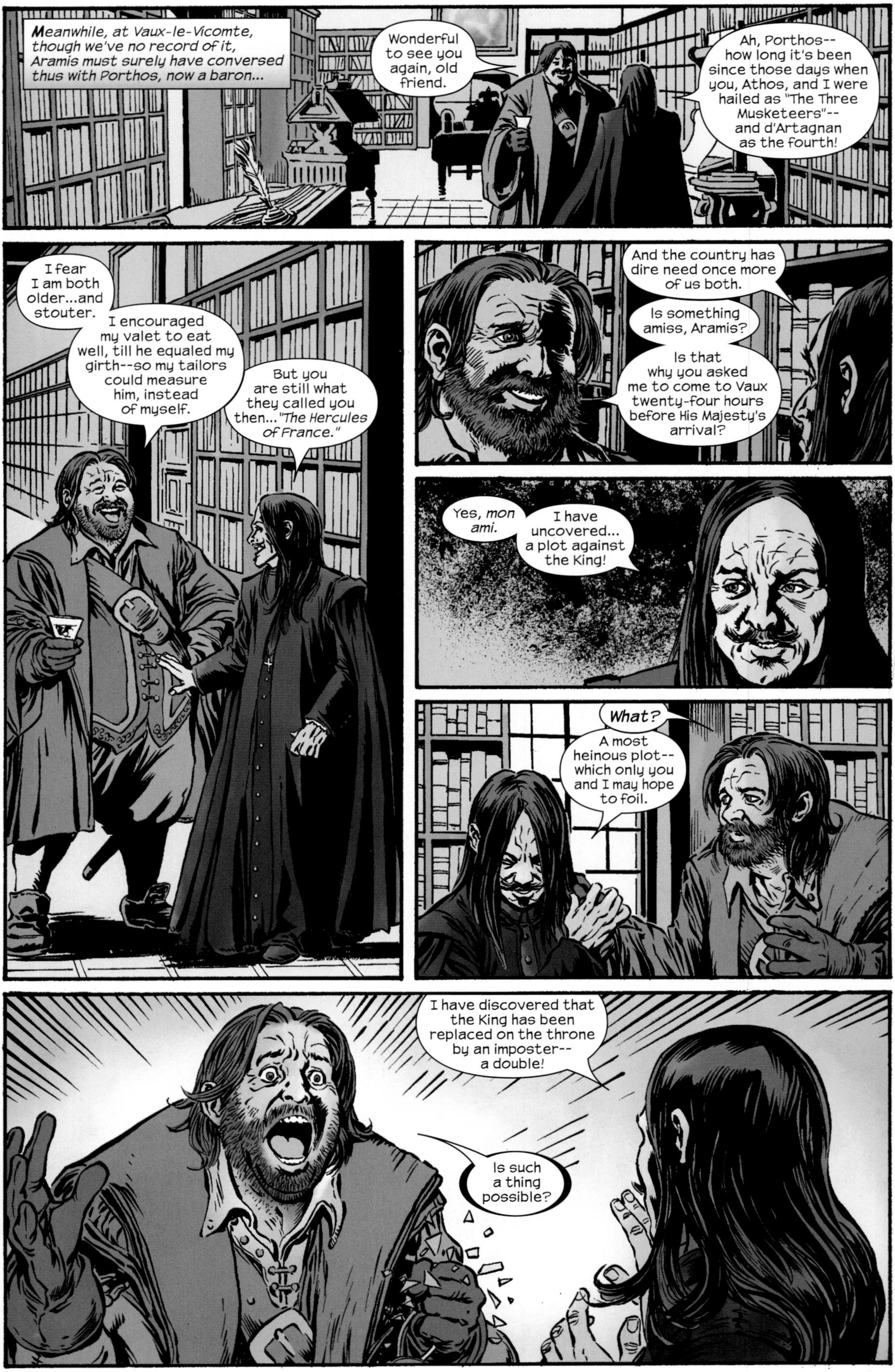
Meanwhile, at Vaux-le-Vicomte, though we've no record of it, Aramis must surely have conversed thus with Porthos, now a baron...
Wonderful to see you again, old friend.
Ah, Porthos-- how long it's been since those days when you, Athos, and I were hailed as "The Three Musketeers"-- and d'Artagnan as the fourth!
I fear I am both older...and stouter.
I encouraged my valet to eat well, till he equaled my girth--so my tailors could measure him, instead of myself.
But you are still what they called you then... "The Hercules of France."
And the country has dire need once more of us both.
Is something amiss, Aramis?
Is that why you asked me to come to Vaux twenty-four hours before His Majesty's arrival?
Yes, mon ami.
I have uncovered... a plot against the King!
What?
A most heinous plot-- which only you and I may hope to foil.
I have discovered that the King has been replaced on the throne by an imposter-- a double!
Is such a thing possible?

Not just possible. Accomplished!

And you and I must place the crown again upon the proper brow.

What must I do to help?

When the time comes, you must obey my commands without question.

Yes, my friend... certainly.

Without question!

Together, we will save the King--and France!

Ah, to be again the champion of France--as in the old days!

Men may yet erect a statue of me--

--and, of course, of you, as well, dear Aramis!

At seven o'clock in the evening, without announcing his arrival by the din of trumpets, and without most of his advance guard...

...the King presented himself before the magnificent gates of Vaux...

...where M. and Mme. Fouquet had been waiting for the last half-hour.

You have had the roads put in excellent order, M. Fouquet.

A stone is hardly to be found the size of an egg the whole way from Mêlun to Vaux, Your Majesty.

I wished it to be as if your carriage were rolling along upon a carpet.

And so, indeed, it was, sir.

At once, any lingering suspicions that d'Artagnan may have had concerning Fouquet's motives disappeared.

"M. Fouquet," he said to himself, "is the man for me."

We do not intend to describe the grand banquet, at which all the royal guests were present, including M. Colbert...though not the Bishop of Vannes or the Baron Porthos.

It will suffice to note that the King's countenance soon went, from being gay, to wearing a gloomy and irritated expression.

He remembered that his own residence, royal though it was, was merely an historical monument of earlier days, the relic of his predecessors.

Fouquet ate from a gold service, and drank wines of which the King of France did not even know the name...

...out of goblets each more precious than the whole royal cellar.

Louis' eyes filled with tears.

He dared not look at his Queen.

When the supper was finished, the King expressed a desire to walk in the illuminated park...

...accompanied only by d'Artagnan and M. Fouquet.

And now the fête was complete in every respect...

...for the King was able to have a "chance encounter" with La Vallière...

...to walk a little while with her in one of the winding paths of the wood...

...and press her hand...

I love you.

...without anyone overhearing him...

...except, of course, for d'Artagnan and M. Fouquet.

The night of magical enchantments stole on.

While the Queens passed to their own apartments, accompanied by the music of theorbos and lutes...

Let me show you, Your Majesty, to your own bedroom...

...the chamber of Morpheus.

M. d'Herbay* oversaw totally the redesign of this part of the château.

I hope you will enjoy the vaulted ceiling, painted by the famous Lebrun...

*Aramis' formal name.

...and depicting the happy, as well as disagreeable, dreams with which that legendary god of sleep affects kings as well as other men.

You shiver, Your Majesty. Is the room too cold?

I...am sleepy, that is all.

Still...would you have the goodness to tell M. Colbert I wish to see him?

Of course, sire.

D'Artagnan, for his part, determined to lose no time in finding his former comrade, the Bishop of Vannes...

...in that worthy's own chamber, called the Blue Room...

Well, Aramis...

...and so we have come to Vaux.

Ah d'Artagnan! I have been engaged about the theatrical performances to take place tomorrow.

SNOORRRR

But--should we go elsewhere? Our friend Porthos is sleeping....

People may talk in the midst of that loud bass snore without fear of disturbing him.

You are the comptroller-general of the fêtes here, then?

You know I am a friend of all kinds of amusement wherein the exercise of imagination is required.

For which reason, I must be close to the King.

The flooring of my room is merely the covering of his ceiling.

Aramis...I must voice what I feel. I fear you conspire against the King.

What? If I have not the firm intention of making tomorrow the most glorious day my King has ever enjoyed--may Heaven's lightning blast me where I stand!

Then why did you take some patterns of His Majesty's costumes from his tailor?

So I could have an accurate portrait of the King painted and present it here.

You will see it on the morrow.

The earnestness of your words soothes my heart. I take my leave.

Please wake Porthos and take him with you...for he snores like a park of artillery.

I shall.

SNORRR

Good night, my friends. In ten minutes I shall be fast asleep.

As soon as his two former comrades had left, Aramis bolted the door...

Monseigneur! Monseigneur!

M. d'Artagnan entertains a great many suspicions, it seems.

Philippe pushed aside a sliding panel behind the bed...

He is very devoted to...me.

If d'Artagnan does not recognize you before the other has disappeared...

...you may rely upon him to the end of the world!

Now, my lord, take up your post at our place of observation...

...and watch the King's actions...

...through these openings.

They answer to one of the false windows...

"...which I caused to be made..."

"...in the dome of the King's apartment."

"Bishop! He has a visitor--I recognize the finance minister!"

This letter, written by the late Cardinal Mazarin, will prove to Your Majesty that thirteen million livres have been given to M. Fouquet.

A tolerably good sum, Colbert.

These thirteen millions have never been returned...

...for M. Fouquet used them to erect this great estate.

They are, no doubt, paying for this very fête.

Mazarin's letter proves it so, Majesty.

If this is true...

It is late. By morning, I shall have made up my mind what to do about M. Fouquet.

But...

Very good, sire.

"The King has given himself time for reflection..."

Now watch, monseigneur, and study well...

...how a King retires to his rest.

History has told us of the various events of the following day and night... of the splendid fêtes given by the Surintendant to his sovereign.

There was a promenade... a banquet...a comedy to be acted.

Full of preoccupation, however, the King showed himself cold, reserved, and taciturn.

Nothing could smooth the frown upon his face...

M. Fouquet observed that deep resentment, rising from the depths of the King's heart...

...and was sorely troubled.

Later that evening, the King and M. Colbert walked in the park...

...where La Vallière contrived to meet her loving sovereign.

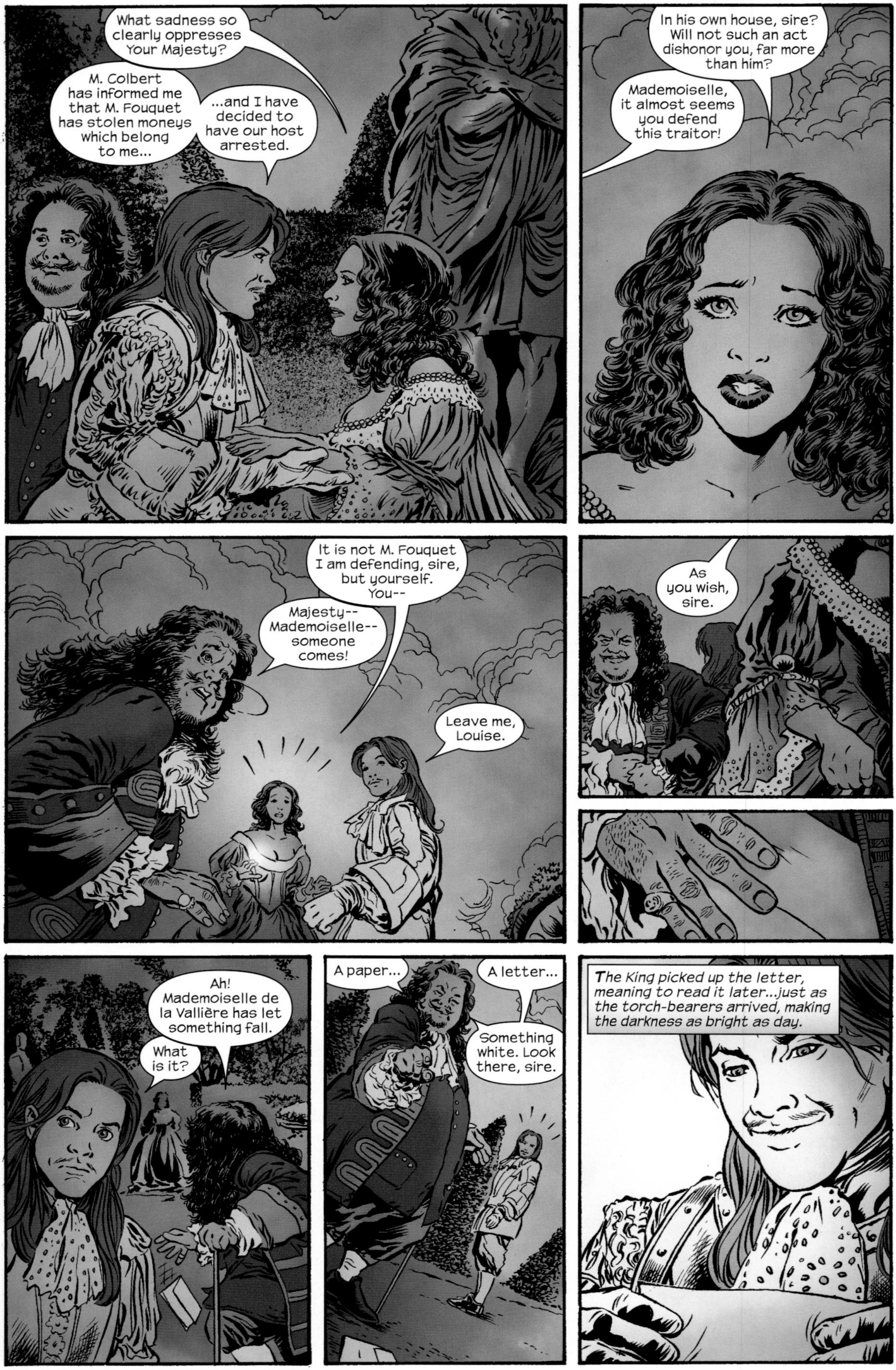
What sadness so clearly oppresses Your Majesty?
M. Colbert has informed me that M. Fouquet has stolen moneys which belong to me...
...and I have decided to have our host arrested.
In his own house, sire? Will not such an act dishonor you, far more than him?
Mademoiselle, it almost seems you defend this traitor!
It is not M. Fouquet I am defending, sire, but yourself. You--
Majesty-- Mademoiselle-- someone comes!
Leave me, Louise.
As you wish, sire.
Ah! Mademoiselle de la Vallière has let something fall.
What is it?
A paper...
A letter...
Something white. Look there, sire.
The King picked up the letter, meaning to read it later...just as the torch-bearers arrived, making the darkness as bright as day.

Hardly had the King returned to the château, than a mass of fire burst from the dome of Vaux, illuminating the remotest corners.

The fireworks had begun.

A death-like pallor stole over his face... as he read a love letter, sent by M. Fouquet to La Vallière, long before...

...and which had recently fallen into-- and from--the hands of M. Colbert.

Ere long, the King remembered the letter...

...which, he believed, La Vallière had dropped as she hurried away.

Minutes afterward, d'Artagnan entered Louis XIV's apartment.

How many men will be required to arrest M. Fouquet?

Arrest M. Fouquet? It is so easy that a mere child might do it.

Still, Your Majesty will forgive me, but, in order to effect this arrest...

...I should like written instructions...

...in case, when your anger passes, you regret your actions.

Since when has the King's word been insufficient for you?

Arrest him, and hold him until the morning...

...when I shall have made up my mind what I shall do with him!

I...will do as you command, sire.

After d'Artagnan had quitted the room...

Fouquet squanders my finances...

...and now tries to rob me of the one to whom I am most attached!

I hate him-- I hate him-- I hate him!

Tomorrow, people shall see what utter ruin a King's anger shall have wrought!

Almost weeping, he threw himself upon his bed...

...and soon, absolute silence reigned in the chamber of Morpheus.

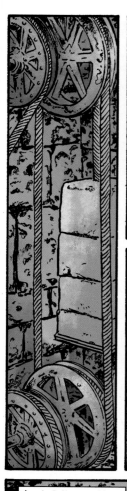

Then it seemed to the King...

...as if the dome...

...gradually receded...

...and that the painted figures...

...became darker and darker...

...as the distance became more and more remote.

Louis felt a gentle, easy movement of the bed, as regular as that by which a vessel plunges beneath the waves...

I am under the influence of a terrible dream...

As the last light of the royal chamber faded away, as if he were descending toward the bottom of a well...

And then the bed stopped.

It is time to awaken from this dream.

Come! Let me wake up!

And then he perceived that he was already awake...

...and that two men, each masked, stood silently at his bedside.

What is this, monsieur?

What is the meaning of this jest?

It is no jest.

Do you belong to M. Fouquet?

It matters very little to whom we belong.

We are your masters now--that is sufficient.

Is this--a dungeon?

No...a subterranean passage.

Will you be good enough to follow us?

I shall not stir from hence!

If you are obstinate, my dear young friend...

I will lift you up in my arms and roll you up in a cloak.

And if you are stifled there, why, so much the worse for you!

It seems... I have fallen into the hands of a pair of assassins.

Tell me, at least, where we are going.

Come.

Unnhh! You dare to shove me thus?

What do you intend to do with the King of France?

Try to forget that word.

You deserve to be broken on the wheel for using that word... but the King is too kind-hearted.

Get in.

In the early hours of the morning, after having called out to the sentinel, "By the King's order!"...

...the driver conducted the horses into the circular enclosure of the Bastille.

THWAM THWAM THWAM

What is the matter now?

Who have you...

...brought me?

Monsieur d'Herblay!

Hush. Let us go inside.

And fire at once if he speaks!

Very good!

Dear Bishop--Aramis--what brings you here at this hour?

It appears, my dear M. de Baisemeaux, that you were quite right the other evening.

We both thought it called for the release of Marchiali...

But, as you see, it is that poor Scotch fellow Seldon whom the King wishes set at liberty.

Indeed, so it says! But you convinced me the order referred to Marchiali.

I am a lost man--releasing the wrong prisoner!

No. Since I have brought Marchiali back, it is as if he had never left.

You will lock him up at once-- and you will release Seldon. Do you understand?

Very good.

I--I--

The man in the carriage-- who did not speak for fear of being shot--was quickly brought into the Bastille...

...and locked in the very cell in which Philippe had, for six long years, bemoaned his existence.

You noticed the resemblance between that unfortunate wretch and--

And the King? Yes!

Well, the very first use he made of his freedom was to dress himself like the King-- and pretend he *was* the King!

Gracious Heavens! I shall go set Seldon free...

Tomorrow will be time enough.

Remember-- no one is to enter Marchiali's cell, except with an order from the King--

--an order I will myself bring.

Now, Porthos, my good fellow... Back again to Vaux, and as fast as possible!

A man is light and easy enough, when he has faithfully served his King...

...and, in serving him, saved his country!

Thus did the young King come to pass the night in the chill of the dungeon...

...even as Philippe lay in restful sleep at Vaux-le-Vicomte...

...beneath the royal canopy.

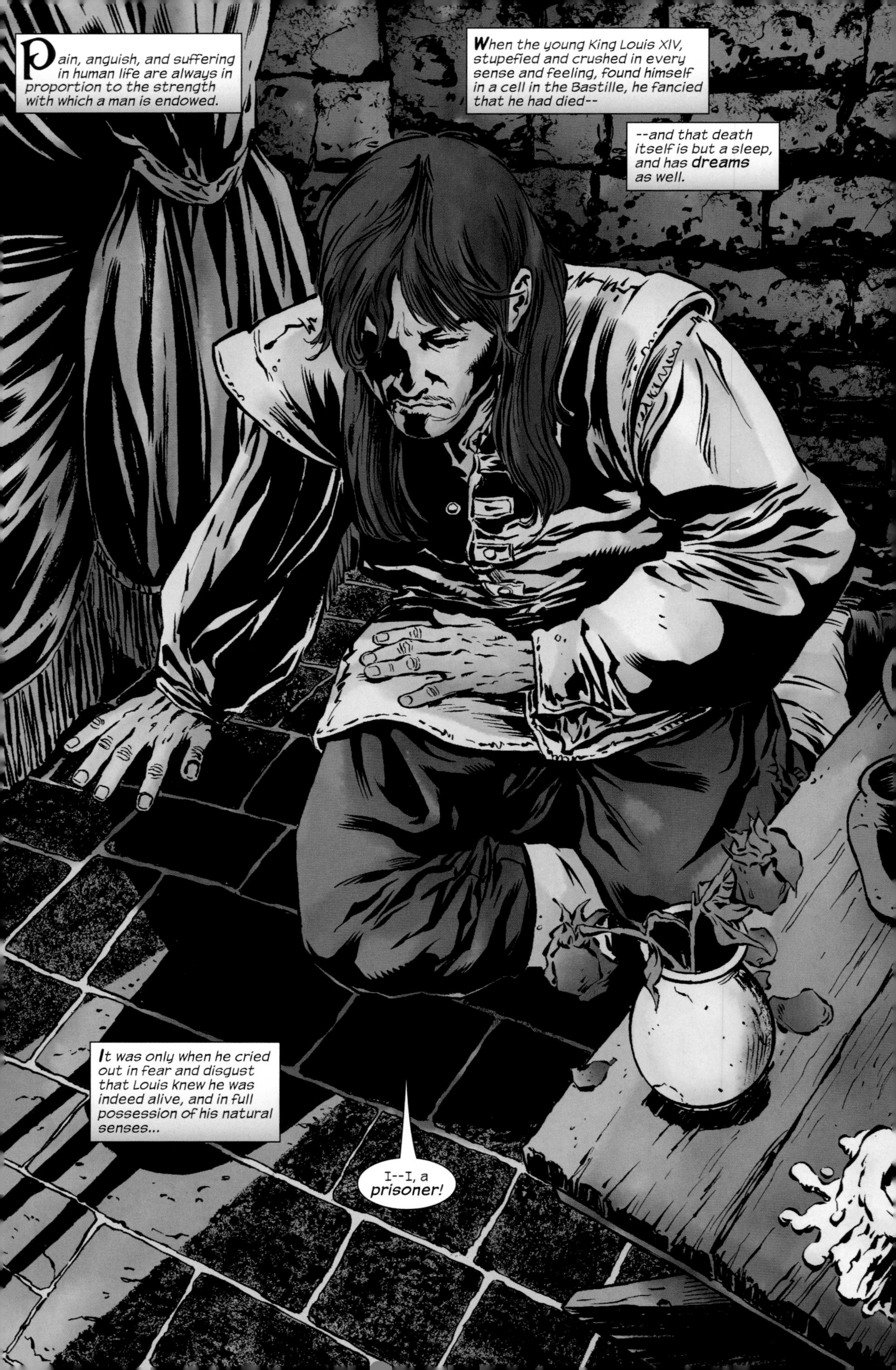
Pain, anguish, and suffering in human life are always in proportion to the strength with which a man is endowed.
When the young King Louis XIV, stupefied and crushed in every sense and feeling, found himself in a cell in the Bastille, he fancied that he had died--
--and that death itself is but a sleep, and has dreams as well.
It was only when he cried out in fear and disgust that Louis knew he was indeed alive, and in full possession of his natural senses...
I--I, a prisoner!

Colbert was right-- Monsieur Fouquet must have drawn me to Vaux, as into a snare.

But he cannot have been acting alone.

I recognized the voice of M. d'Herblay beneath that mask.

There is a governor in this place.

I will summon him to me!

The shattering of the chair awakened many a mournful echo in the profound depths of the staircase...

SMASH

...but from a human creature, not one.

This was a fresh proof for the King of the slight regard in which he was held at the Bastille.

Remarking a barred window...

...Louis began to call out, at first gently enough... ...then louder, and louder still.

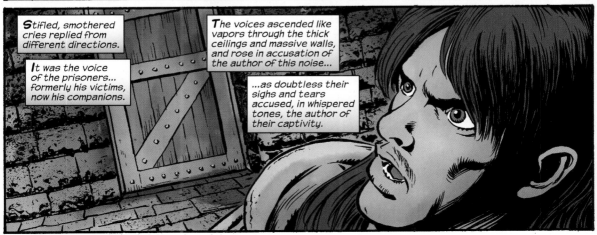

Stifled, smothered cries replied from different directions.

It was the voice of the prisoners... formerly his victims, now his companions.

The voices ascended like vapors through the thick ceilings and massive walls, and rose in accusation of the author of this noise...

...as doubtless their sighs and tears accused, in whispered tones, the author of their captivity.

After having deprived so many people of their liberty...

...the King now came among them to rob them of their rest.

This idea almost drove him mad.

What is the matter with you this morning?

Monsieur-- are you the governor of the Bastille?

You have always been very quiet and reasonable, Marchiali--but you are getting vicious, it seems.

There is no reason why you should make such a terrible disturbance.

Desire the governor to come to me!

If I even thought of disturbing him...

...he would merely send you off to one of the lower dungeons.

Two hours afterward, Louis could not have been recognized as a king...

...a gentleman...

...a human being.

He might, rather, be called a madman.

And so the bright orb of approaching day shone down upon the hated Bastille...

...and upon the singular magnificence of the Château de Vaux-le-Vicomte.

Philippe had slept uneasily, sheltered beneath his stolen crown.

Then, towards the morning...

...a shadow, rather than a body, glided into the royal chamber...

Well, M. d'Herblay?

Well, sire, all is done. The governor of the Bastille suspected nothing.

The resemblance between us, however--

That was the cause of the success.

In a few days, we will send the captive to a place of exile so distant that the duration of human life would not be enough to allow his return.

And what is to be done with the Baron du Vallon?*

Why... confer a dukedom upon him, I suppose.

*Porthos.

A step... in the vestibule...

Louis bade my Captain of the Musketeers arrest M. Fouquet, and report here at the break of day.

D'Artagnan is a most punctual man.

But if he enters this room this morning, he will be sure to detect something that happened here.

But how can I send him away, since "I" have given him the rendezvous?

I will take care of that.

NOK NOK

Good morning, dear d'Artagnan.

Aramis! You here?

His Majesty desires you to report that he is still sleeping, after having been greatly fatigued during the whole night.

I have here an order of His Majesty, which concerns M. Fouquet.

I will go with you, for I wish to be a witness of his delight.

I am *free!?*

Yes, M. Fouquet... by the King's order. You may thank the Bishop of Vannes, for it is to him that you owe the change that has taken place in His Majesty.

But how, Aramis, have you managed to become the King's favorite--you who have never spoken to him more than twice in your life?

Ah, the fact is that I have seen him more than a hundred times...only we have kept it very secret.

Then, perceiving that Aramis and Fouquet desired to speak in private, d'Artagnan took his leave...

Now, my dear d'Herblay, I think you should explain...

...why the King has set me at liberty, when only last night he ordered my arrest?

Colbert had convinced him I was a thief...nor did the King like *you*, I know.

The King will like me *now.*

Nor will he be, any longer, your powerful and implacable enemy.

But what happened to change things?

Do you remember the birth of Louis XIV?

This is where my secret begins.

The Queen, you must know, instead of being delivered of one son, was delivered of *two*.

What? And the second is dead?

No. Both the children grew up--the one on the throne--

--the other, brought up in the country, then thrown into the Bastille at the age of fifteen.

The King's mother, Anne of Austria, knew it all... the King, absolutely nothing.

Ah, now I understand!

You threatened to reveal that secret, and that is why you now have the King in your power!

You understand nothing as yet.

God had formed these twins so miraculously like each other that it would be utterly impossible to distinguish the one from the other.

"Yet one has sat upon the throne of France these past several years...

"...while the other, who is, most incontestably, superior in every way to his brother, has been a prisoner of the Bastille.

There is a further inequality between them, which concerns yourself.

Between those twin sons of Louis XIII, the one who has been in prison does not know M. Colbert.

I understand you now, at last.

You are proposing a conspiracy to me?

You propose that I should agree to the substitution of one son of Louis XIII for another upon the throne?

It is already done.

The King of yesterday has gone to take his place in the Bastille which his victim has occupied for such a long time past.

And you committed such an action--here, at my own home?

Here at Vaux, in the Chamber of Morpheus.

Last night, between twelve and one o'clock.

You have *dishonored* me in committing so foul an act of treason--so heinous a crime!

He was my guest--my sovereign--peacefully reposing beneath my roof!

Have I a man out of his senses to deal with here?

You have an *honorable man* to deal with.

You are mad! A man who will prevent you from consummating your crime.

A man who would far sooner die--who would *kill you,* even--rather than allow you to complete his dishonor!

Reflect, monseigneur, upon everything we have to expect.

As the matter now stands, the King is still alive, and his imprisonment saves your life.

You may have been acting on my behalf--but I do not accept your services.

Yet, I do not wish your ruin...

You will leave this house.

You must leave *France!*

Upon the word of Fouquet, no one--not even the King's men--shall follow you before the expiration of four hours' time.

Four hours?

It is more time than you will need to get on board a vessel and flee to *Belle-Isle*...which I give you as a place of refuge.

Go, d'Herblay--go! As long as I live, not a hair of your head shall be injured.

Aramis replied with a cold irony of manner.

Thank you.

Now we both must hasten away--you to save your life, I to save my honor.

As Fouquet hurried off to order his best horses, Aramis knew he could not warn Philippe and take him along to Belle-Isle...

Else war would follow-- civil war, implacable in its nature.

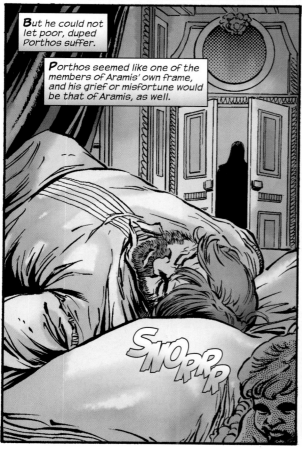

But he could not let poor, duped Porthos suffer.

Porthos seemed like one of the members of Aramis' own frame, and his grief or misfortune would be that of Aramis, as well.

SNORRR

Come, Porthos... come.

We are going off... mounted, and faster than we have ever gone in our lives.

Ahh...?

Porthos obeyed, rising from his bed even before his intelligence seemed to be aroused...and Aramis helped the giant to dress himself...

What the devil are you doing there in such an agitated manner?

We are going off on a mission of great importance, d'Artagnan.

I would far sooner be fast asleep...but the service of the King...

I have seen M. Fouquet, this very minute, ride off in a carriage.

What did he say to you?

Adieu...nothing more. Am I worth his speaking to, now that you have got into such high favor?

I predict that something will happen today which will increase your importance more than ever.

D'Artagnan gazed after his two old friends until they were out of sight.

They were going on a mission, they said...

But they looked more as if they were making an escape.

All the while, Fouquet tore along toward Paris as fast as his horses could drag him...even as he trembled with horror at what had just been revealed to him...

*What must have been, he thought, the **youth** of those extraordinary men, who, even as age is stealing fast upon them, still are able to conceive such plans...*

...and carry them out without flinching?

The Surintendant arrived at the Bastille, having traveled at the rate of five leagues and a half per hour.

Baisemeaux, governor of the prison, recognized him immediately.

But he had his orders...

Monseigneur, you know that no one can see any of the prisoners without an express order from the King.

You will let me see the prisoner called Marchiali-- *now*--

--or I will return at the head of ten thousand men and thirty pieces of cannon!

C-come with me to the keep, monseigneur, and you shall see him at once.

This job will *kill* me, I am sure it will!

Minutes later, the door to a certain cell flew open...

The King-- in this state!?

Monsieur Fouquet...

Have you come to assassinate me?

Sire--do you not recognize the most faithful of your friends--the most respectful of your servants?

A friend-- *you!*

My King--how you must have suffered!

Come, sire. You are free... and will be at the head of an army of ten thousand in an hour.

Free?

You set me at liberty, after having dared to lift up your hand against me?

*T*hen, rapidly, Fouquet related the whole particulars of the intrigue... and how all from the Baisemeaux to himself had been deceived.

*S*oon, though with difficulty, the King was convinced...

...though he scowled to learn Fouquet had given them four hours' head start for impregnable Belle-Isle.

Come, M. Fouquet.

I am at Your Majesty's orders... but I think Your Majesty can hardly dispense with changing your clothes previous to appearing before your court.

We shall pass by the Louvre.

Baisemeaux looked completely bewildered as he saw Marchiali once more leave the Bastille...

...and, in his helplessness, he tore out the few remaining hairs he had left.

In the meantime, usurped royalty was playing out its part bravely at Vaux.

Determined to try his valor and his fortune notwithstanding the absence of Mr. d'Herblay, Philippe gave orders for a full reception of his court.

He had watched, the evening before, all the habits of his brother...and now played the King in such a manner as to awaken no suspicion.

His own memory, and the notes prepared for him by Aramis, announced everyone to him...

...though he was glad that his "wife," the Queen, was feeling poorly and was not present.

He smiled at seeing all these countenances so familiar to him...

...none of which he had ever seen before.

He contemplated his brother, M. de Saint-Aignan, who had usurped nothing from him.

Philippe promised himself to be a kind brother to this Prince who required nothing but gold to minister to his pleasures...

...and he tremblingly held out his hand to Henrietta, his sister-in-law, whose beauty struck him.

Yet he saw in the eyes of that Princess an expression of coldness.

Then, his mother, Anne of Austria, began a dissertation on the welcome M. Fouquet had given to the House of France, mixing hostilities with compliments...

Well, my son...are you convinced with regard to M. Fouquet and his thieving?

Madame, I do not like to hear M. Fouquet ill-spoken of.

It is a fact-- he is ruining the State.

I will hear no more concerning *pretended robberies* the Surintendant is falsely said to have committed.

Mother, I wish only for you to make your peace with M. Fouquet.

The Queen-Mother did not realize that, in that kiss, there was a pardon for six years of horrible suffering.

What is Your Majesty looking for? Your eyes turn constantly toward the door.

My sister, I am expecting a most distinguished man...

...a most able counselor, whom I wish to present to all, recommending him to your good graces.

Ah! Come in then, d'Artagnan.

What does Your Majesty wish?

I am waiting for your friend, the Bishop of Vannes. Let him be sought for.

D'Artagnan, reflecting that Aramis had left upon a mission, concluded that the King wished to preserve the secret of it.

Sire...does Your Majesty absolutely require M. d'Herblay to be brought to you?

No...but if he can be found...

This way! This way! A few steps more, sire!

Ah! The voice of M. Fouquet.

Then M. d'Herblay cannot be far off.

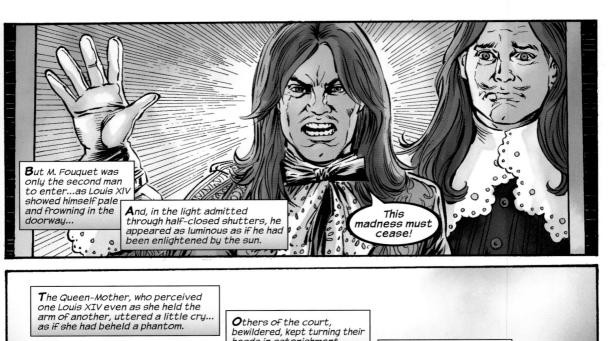

But M. Fouquet was only the second man to enter...as Louis XIV showed himself pale and frowning in the doorway...

And, in the light admitted through half-closed shutters, he appeared as luminous as if he had been enlightened by the sun.

This madness must cease!

The Queen-Mother, who perceived one Louis XIV even as she held the arm of another, uttered a little cry... as if she had beheld a phantom.

Others of the court, bewildered, kept turning their heads in astonishment from one to the other...

...or thought they saw the form of the King somehow reflected in a glass...

...as the two Louises measured each other with their looks, and darted their eyes into each other like poniards.

Yet, even then, Anne of Austria did not guess the truth...

...and others could not know it.

My mother, do you not acknowledge your *son*--

--since everyone here has forgotten his *King*?

But Philippe, even in drawing back, responded with a calm voice...

My mother--

--do you not acknowledge your *son*?

Please... I...

Ooohhhh...

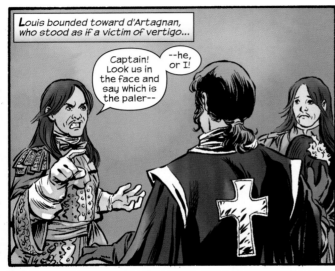

Louis bounded toward d'Artagnan, who stood as if a victim of vertigo...

Captain! Look us in the face and say which is the paler--

--he, or I!

Then, without hesitation, d'Artagnan walked straight up to Philippe...

Monsieur...

You are my prisoner!

Casting down his eyes against Philippe's reproachful stare, Louis led M. de Sainte-Aignan and his wife from the room...

...as Philippe approached Anne of Austria.

If I were not your son, I should curse you, my mother, for having rendered me...

...so unhappy.

Excuse me, monseigneur. I am but a soldier, and my oaths are his who has just left the chamber.

Thank you, M. d'Artagnan. But what is become of M. d'Herblay?

M. d'Herblay is in safety, monseigneur...

...and no one, while I live and am free, shall cause a hair to fall from his head.

M. Fouquet...

Pardon me, monseigneur, but he who has just gone out was my guest.

Here are brave friends and good hearts.

They make me regret the world.

On, M. d'Artagnan. I follow you.

At that moment, M. Colbert appeared in the doorway...

M. d'Artagnan...

...I have come to remit to you an order from the King.

What is it?

Read, monseigneur.

M. d'Artagnan will conduct the prisoner to the Ile Sainte-Marguerite.

He will cover his face with an iron visor, which the prisoner cannot raise without peril to his life.

Louis

That is just.

I am ready.

Aramis was right, d'Artagnan. This one is quite as much of a king as the other.

More, M. Fouquet! He only wants you and me.

Aramis and Porthos, having profited by the time granted them by Fouquet, did honor to the French Cavalry by their speed...

...and were already more than a dozen leagues from Vaux...

I do not understand, Aramis, why we are forced to display so much velocity.

Hush, old friend...

Know only that our fortune depends upon our speed.

That magic word "fortune" always means something in the human ear.

And so Porthos pushed forward, as if he had still been the Musketeer of 1626, without a *sou* or a *maille*.

I shall be a *duke*!

That is possible.

Though Aramis smiled after his own fashion, his head was, notwithstanding, on fire...

...even though the fugitives were five hours in advance of any possible pursuers.

After eight long hours, they had arrived at Orleans and changed horses.

They rode on twenty leagues more, and at evening reached another post.

...where, alas...

A thousand apologies, monseigneur...

...but there are no horses at this post at present.

Find me two horses so I may pay a visit to a nobleman of my acquaintance who resides near this place...

...the Count de la Fère.*

*Athos, third of the famed Three Musketeers.

All my horses are engaged by the Duke of Beaufort... but I will harness an old blind horse, who has still his legs left.

Ah! That is worth a *louis*!

The post master, having got the carriage ready, ordered one of his men to drive the stranger to La Fère...

Ah... I understand now, Aramis!

What do you understand?

We are going, on the part of the King, to make some great proposal to Athos.

You need tell me nothing more. I shall guess.

They reached Athos's dwelling about nine o'clock...

Gentlemen, you have arrived.

Even as the two travelers alighted before the gate of the château...

...Athos and his son Raoul were taking comfort in each other's company.

Never shall I accustom myself to the idea that Louise de la Vallière betrayed me for the King.

A woman who would have yielded to a king because he is a king would deserve to be styled infamous.

But Louise loves Louis, Raoul.

Both being young, they have forgotten-- he his rank, and she her vows.

Love absolves everything.

And do not forget the respect due to the King.

The time will come when kings will become less than other men, not more.

You are right. All that you say will happen.

Kings will lose their privileges, as stars which have completed their time lose their splendor.

But when that moment shall come, Raoul, we shall be dead.

In this world, all--men, women, and kings--must live for the present.

We can only live for the future... for God.

BONNG

That bell must signal the arrival of a visitor.

Aramis!

Porthos!

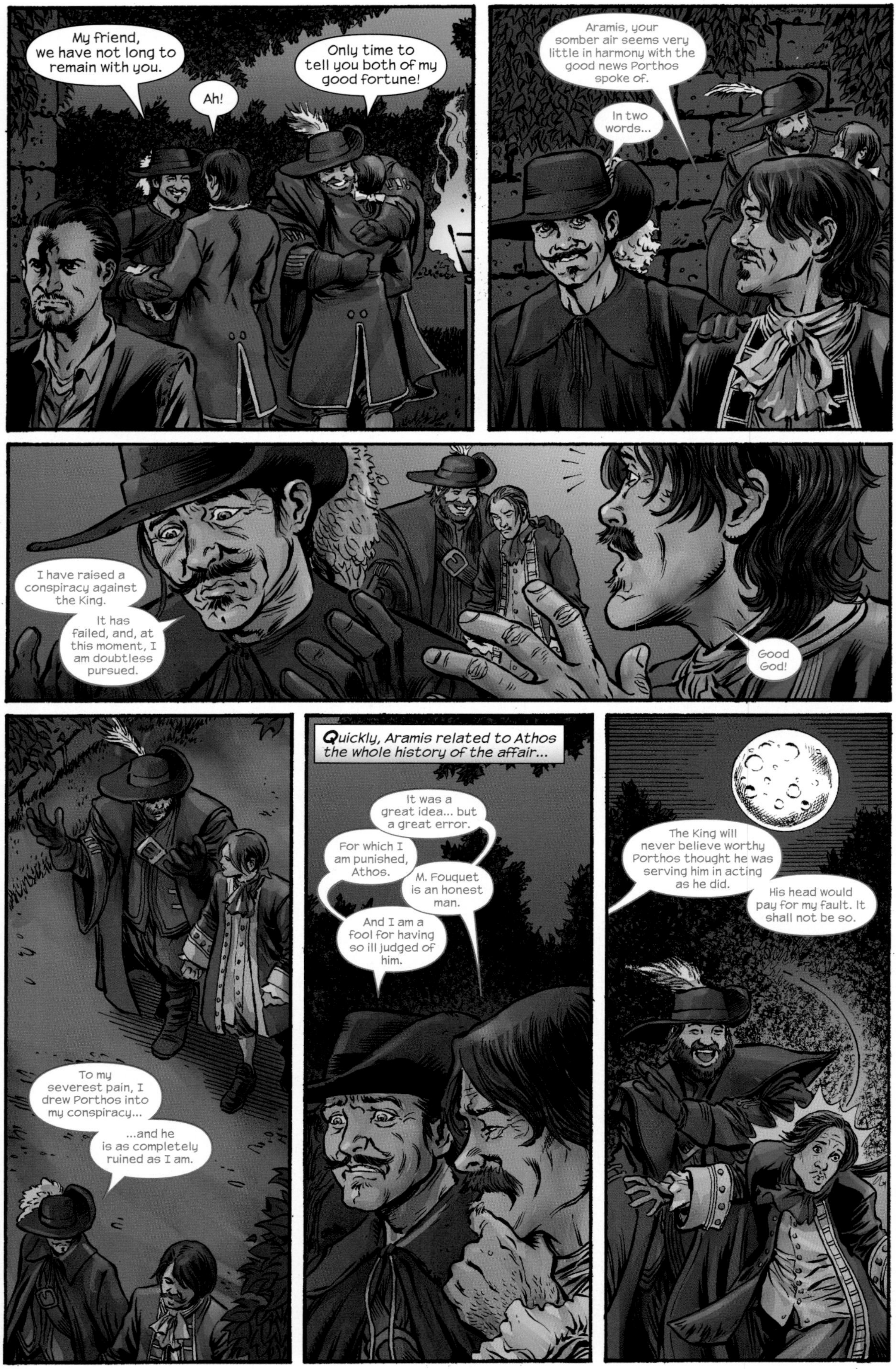
My friend, we have not long to remain with you.
Ah!
Only time to tell you both of my good fortune!
Aramis, your somber air seems very little in harmony with the good news Porthos spoke of.
In two words...
I have raised a conspiracy against the King.
It has failed, and, at this moment, I am doubtless pursued.
Good God!
To my severest pain, I drew Porthos into my conspiracy...
...and he is as completely ruined as I am.
Quickly, Aramis related to Athos the whole history of the affair...
It was a great idea... but a great error.
For which I am punished, Athos.
M. Fouquet is an honest man.
And I am a fool for having so ill judged of him.
The King will never believe worthy Porthos thought he was serving him in acting as he did.
His head would pay for my fault. It shall not be so.

I am taking him to Belle-Isle, at first... which I myself made for Fouqet an impregnable place of refuge.

Then I have a vessel to pass over into England, where I have many relations.

You? In England?

Yes... or else into Spain, where I have still more.

I know how, once abroad, to reconcile myself with Louis XIV, and restore Porthos to favor.

You and Raoul have also griefs to lay to the King.

Follow our example, and pass over into Belle-Isle.

I guarantee that in a month there will be war between France and Spain on the subject of this other son of Louis XIII.

I will intercede, a result which must bring greatness to Porthos and me.

Will you join us?

No, Aramis. I prefer having something to reproach the King with.

Then give me your absolution-- and your two best horses.

You shall have both, old friend.

And when the two fugitives mounted their horses...

...Athos knew that he had seen his two old comrades for the last time.

Later that evening, Raoul startled his father with an unexpected announcement...

Father, in a few weeks I will sail with M. de Beaufort.

He is bound for Africa, to make conquests among the Arabs.

I would wish to keep you here with me, Raoul.

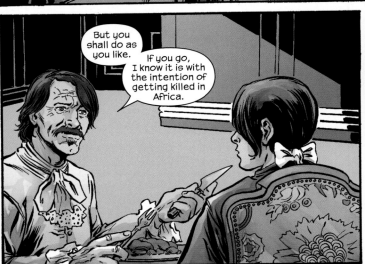

But you shall do as you like.

If you go, I know it is with the intention of getting killed in Africa.

If I do not go...

...I shall die here of grief and love.

The next day, father and son set out upon the road for Fontainebleau... where, they had heard, d'Artagnan had gone on a mysterious mission.

They were determined to find him, that Raoul might pay his final goodbyes to one of his family's firmest friends.

They had lost all traces of d'Artagnan at Antibe, until they spoke with a fisherman...

My boat's been laid up to refit since a trip I made on account of a gentleman who was in great haste to depart.

I pray you, tell me more, my good man.

Six days past, a man came in the night to hire my boat...

...for the purpose of visiting the island of St. Honorat, he said.

The price was agreed upon...

"...but later he returned with an immense carriage case, which he insisted must embark with him.

This is too large for my boat.

I insist. You will carry it on board... *now!*

Nay. I wish to retract our agreement.

Now begone, or my first mate will give you a thrashing!

"My threats, alas, procured me nothing but a shower of blows from the gentleman's cane...

"And I'm not ashamed to say that I fled, swearing and grumbling...

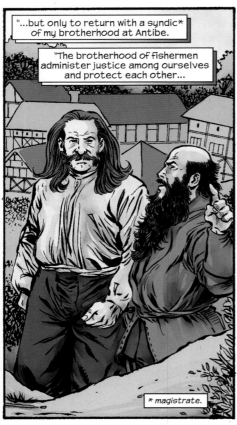

"...but only to return with a syndic* of my brotherhood at Antibe.

"The brotherhood of fishermen administer justice among ourselves and protect each other...

* magistrate.

"But the gentleman exhibited a certain paper...

"...at the sight of which the syndic bowed to the very ground.

Do as the gentleman says, you fool!

"We thus loaded the burdensome freight into my boat...

"...which it nearly filled.

"I was steering toward St. Honorat, when--

I have changed my mind.

I require you to land me instead at Sainte-Marguerite's.

I will take you where we agreed upon-- and nowhere else!

You will do as I say--

--or I shall strangle you.

"To make him pay for such effrontery, I armed myself with a hatchet...

"...as did my first mate.

"But the gentleman drew his sword, and used it in such an astonishingly rapid manner...

"...that we neither of us could get near him.

"I was about to hurl my hatchet at his head--

"--and I had a right to do so, for a sailor aboard is master--

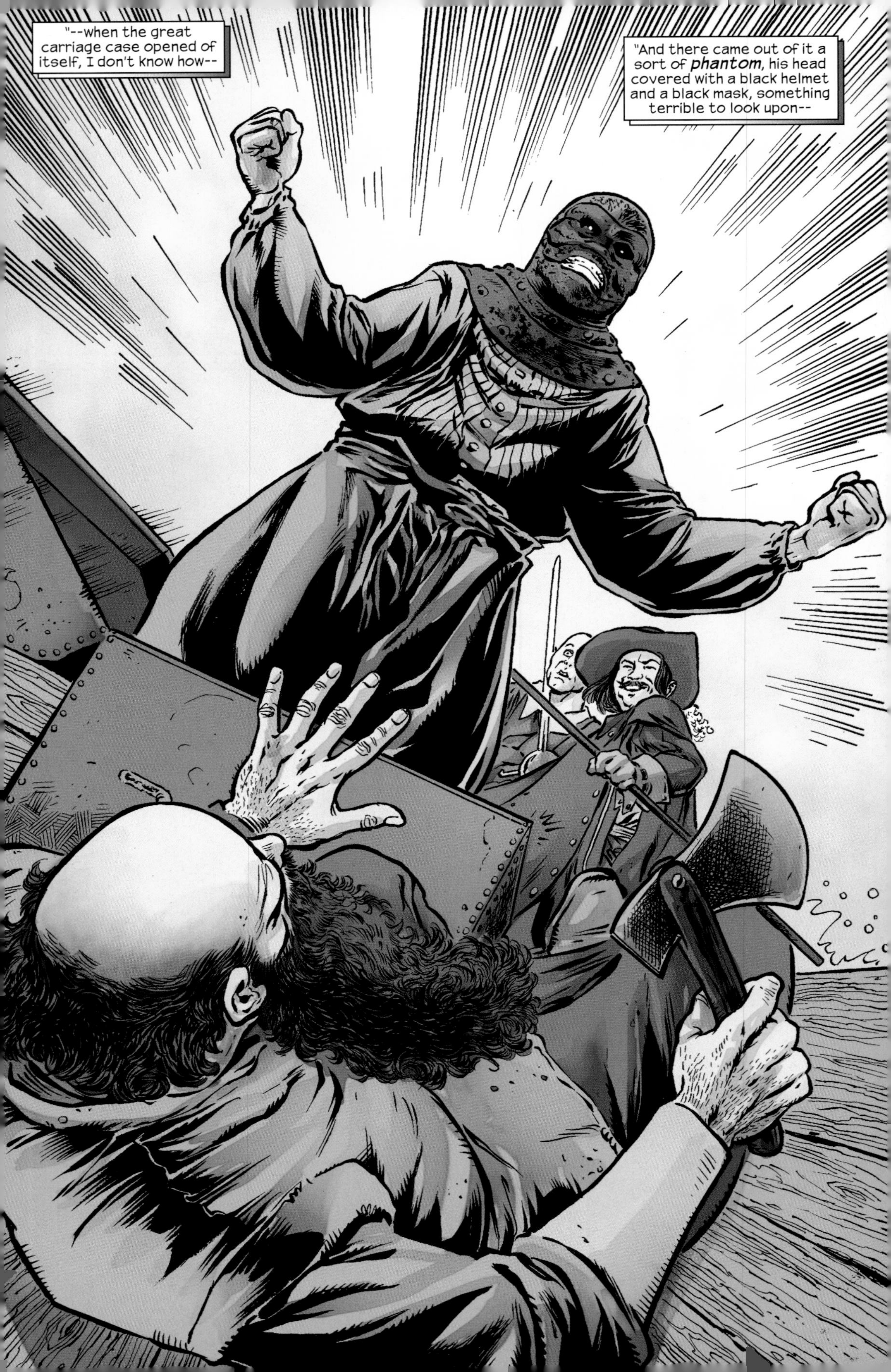
"--when the great carriage case opened of itself, I don't know how--
"And there came out of it a sort of *phantom*, his head covered with a black helmet and a black mask, something terrible to look upon--

"--which came towards me, threatening with its fists!

"Seeing him, the gentleman cried out with great glee...

Ah! Thank you, monseigneur!

"Two poor men, such as we are, could be no match for two gentlemen...

"But, when one of them is the Devil, we had no chance!

"My companion and I did not stop to consult one another...

"We made but one jump into the sea...

"For we were within seven or eight hundred feet of the shore.

"The last we saw, our boat was making for Sainte-Marguerite's.

"When we recovered the boat, we found nothing, not even the carriage case.

"I made my complaint to the governor of Sainte-Marguerite's...

"...who told me if I plagued him with such silly stories, he would have me flogged!"

We will go to Sainte-Marguerite's--for that gentleman very much resembles d'Artagnan...

...and that fisherman's story may conceal some violence those fellows have committed upon their passengers in the open sea.

Who knew whether hatchet or iron bar had not succeeded in doing that which the best blades of Europe, balls, and bullets had not been able to do in forty years?

That same day, Athos and Raoul set out for Sainte-Marguerite's on board a lugger, come from Toulon under orders...

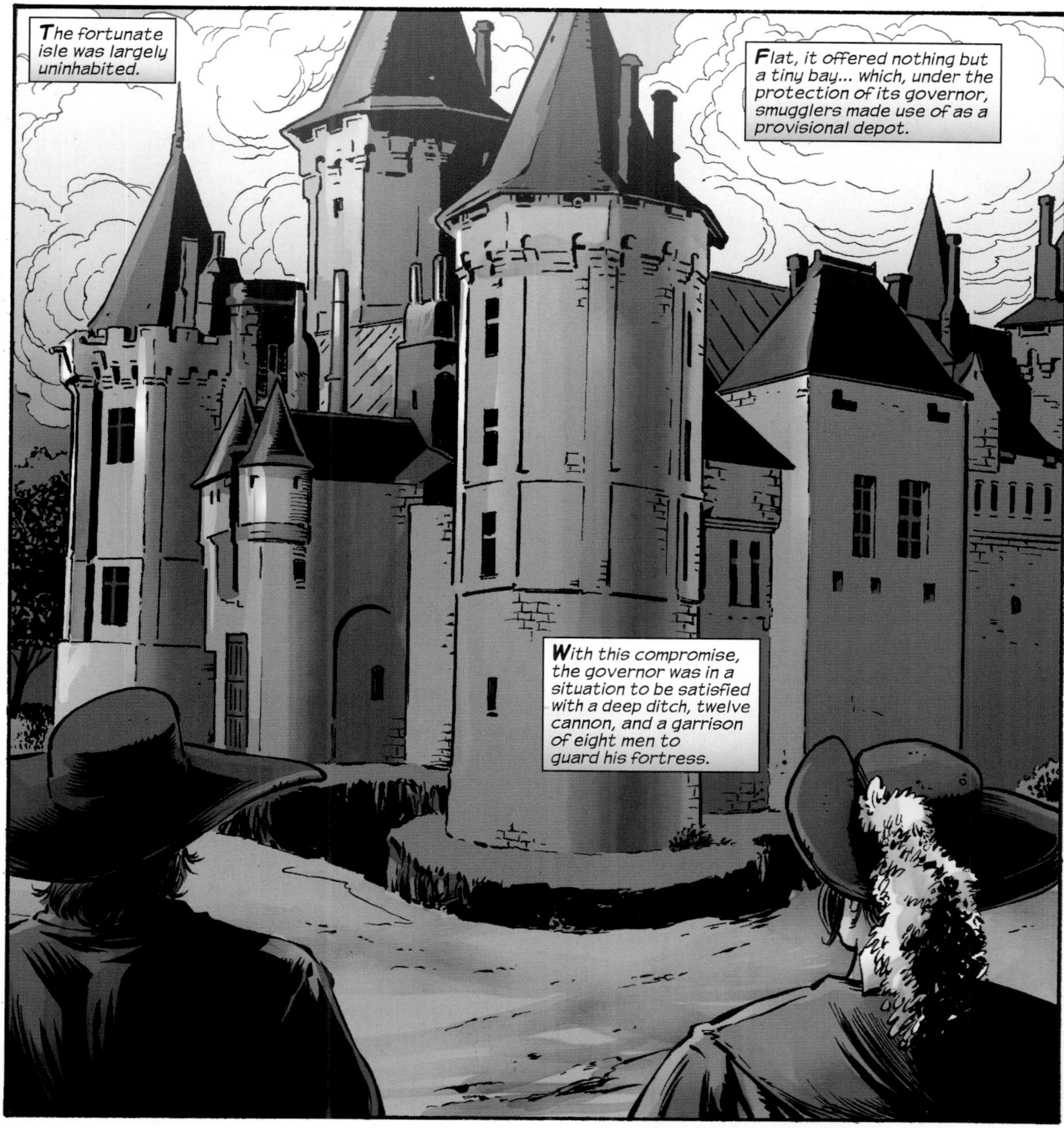
The fortunate isle was largely uninhabited.
Flat, it offered nothing but a tiny bay... which, under the protection of its governor, smugglers made use of as a provisional depot.
With this compromise, the governor was in a situation to be satisfied with a deep ditch, twelve cannon, and a garrison of eight men to guard his fortress.
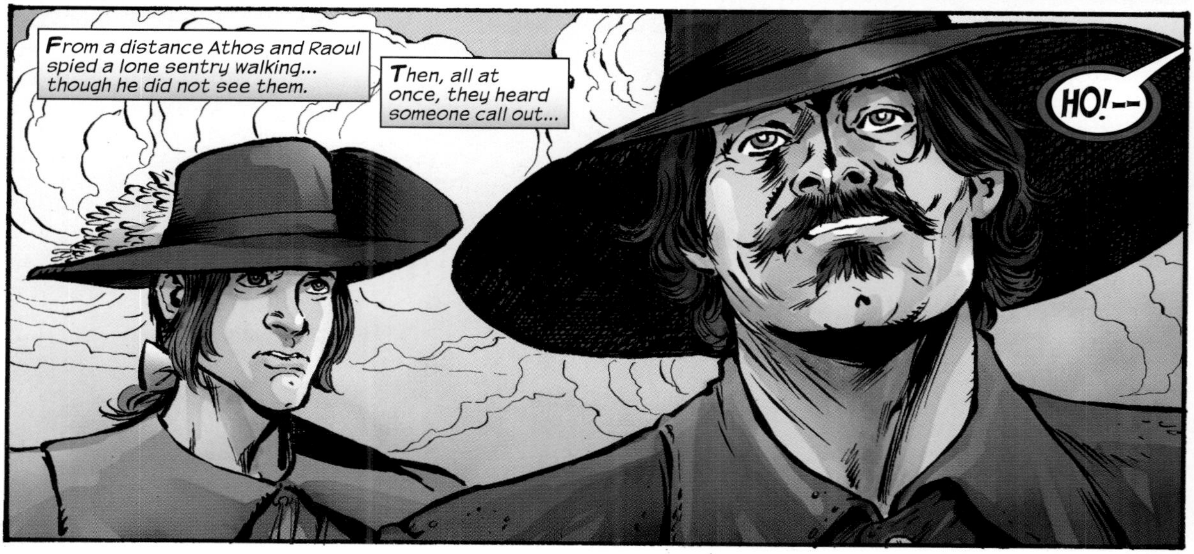
From a distance Athos and Raoul spied a lone sentry walking... though he did not see them.
Then, all at once, they heard someone call out...
HO!--

Raising their heads toward a barred window in one of the turrets, they saw--

THUNK

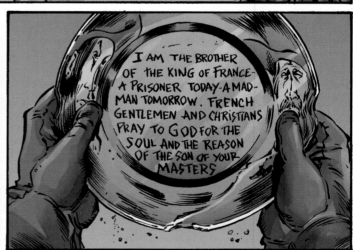

I AM THE BROTHER OF THE KING OF FRANCE- A PRISONER TODAY-A MAD-MAN TOMORROW. FRENCH GENTLEMEN AND CHRISTIANS PRAY TO GOD FOR THE SOUL AND THE REASON OF THE SON OF YOUR MASTERS

What is the *meaning* of these dismal words?

Blackguards!

Father--

BA-LAAM

Get down!

Hnnhh--!

Cordieu! What-- are people assassinated here? Come down, cowards as you are!

Yes-- come down!

Within minutes, the garrison's eight soldiers showed themselves on the other side of the ditch, with their muskets in hand.

At their head was an officer, whom Athos and Raoul recognized as the one who had fired.

Make ready!

We are going to be shot!

Sword in hand, let us leap the ditch and kill at least two of these scoundrels when their muskets are empty.

Yes! We've no choice but to--

Athos! Raoul!

D'Artagnan!

Recover arms! Mordioux!

The captain was crying out to the soldiers beyond the ditch.

What? Were we to be shot without warning?

And *I* would not have missed, my dear friends.

How fortunate it is that I am accustomed to take a long aim--and thought I recognized you.

And the gentleman who fired at us?

Monsieur Saint-Mars--the governor of the fortress.

But why--?

Pardieu! You received what the prisoner threw to you?

This plate--the prisoner has written something on the bottom of it, has he not?

Yes! I feared as much.

Is this our fault? What will this Saint-Mars do to us?

Silence! If he believes you can read-- if he only suspects you have understood--!

Father-- the governor is coming!

Silence! You both are Spaniards-- you do not understand a word of French!

I was right, M. Saint-Mars.

These gentlemen are two Spanish captains with whom I was acquainted at Ypres last year.

They don't know a word of French.

Ah!

And yet they were trying to read the inscription on the plate.

How! What are you doing, M. d'Artagnan?

You have effaced the characters with the point of your sword.

I cannot read them now!

It is a State secret. I will, if you like, allow you to read it--

--and have you *shot* immediately afterwards.

Is it possible that these two do not comprehend at least some words?

Even if they understand a few spoken words, it does not follow that they can understand what is written.

Being noblemen, they cannot even read Spanish.

Very well. Please invite these gentlemen to come to the fortress.

D'Artagnan-- what is this all about?

I have conducted hither a prisoner, whom the King commands shall not be seen.

I was at dinner with the governor when I saw the object thrown, and Raoul pick it up.

I feared my prisoner had written nonsense about his being the rightful King!

D'Artagnan-- we have seen Aramis, a fugitive, ruined--and he has told us all.

A fine secret must be that of which twelve or fifteen persons hold the tattered fragments!

Why have you come to the Isle of Sainte-Marguerite's?

To bid you farewell--for I sail to Africa with M. de Beaufort.

Will you please give this letter to Louise de la Vallière? It says that I love her--and I die.

I shall deliver it, in spite of peril.

Athos-- can you not stop him from going to that land where so many perish?

I am old, my friend. I have no longer courage.

If God takes me from a Raoul--or a d'Artagnan--I should curse him, and a Christian gentleman ought not to curse his God.

It is quite enough to have cursed a king!

Look you! The prisoner is returning from chapel, in the company of the governor.

By red flashes of lightning against the violet fog, they saw a man clothed in black stop, six paces behind the governor...

Come on, monsieur!

Monsieur--!

Say 'Monseigneur'!

What?

Who spoke?

It was I, M. Saint-Mars.

You know that it is the order--that the prisoner be addressed as "my lord" and not merely as "sir."

Call me neither Monsieur or Monseigneur...

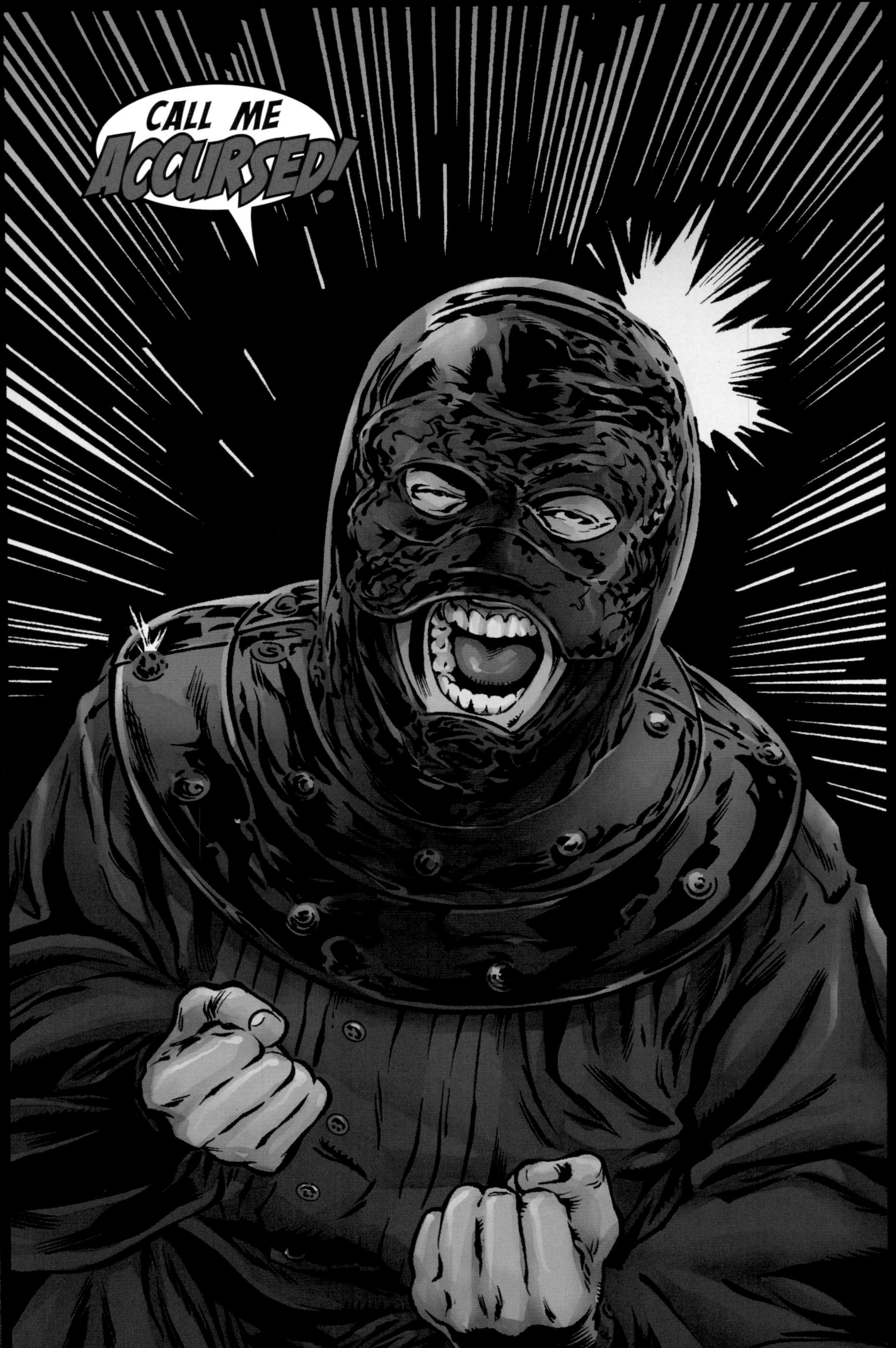
CALL ME ACCURSED!

Then he passed on...

...and the iron door creaked after him.

That is truly an unfortunate man!

Later that same night, d'Artagnan received orders from King Louis to return immediately to Paris, as he had delivered his prisoner.

The three comrades quitted the little isle together, by the last flashes of the departing tempest.

And d'Artagnan feared, when he left them upon the shore at Antibe, that he would see Raoul no more...

...nor even Athos, with whom he had shared so many adventures.

D'artagnan could not smile upon his friends when they parted.

It was, he knew, an evil presage.

A few nights later:

D'Artagnan, accommodating his action to the pace of his horse, employed his thoughts about nothing...

...that is to say, about everything:

Of Philippe, hidden forever beneath a mask of iron...with despair beginning to devour him.

Of fugitive Aramis, soldier and priest...

...who had never taken the good things of this life but as stepping-stones to rise to bad ones.

Of good, harmless Porthos...ruined, yet unsuspecting.

Of Athos, whose son had left France to seek a melancholy death.

Of M. Fouquet, whom King Louis had ordered d'Artagnan to pursue and arrest.

And, later, of finding M. Colbert with the King...

Sire, M. Colbert has ordered my men to pillage M. Fouquet's house.

The King alone has the right to command my Musketeers!

M. Colbert, give me your hand...that I may place it in that of M. d'Artagnan.

M. d'Artagnan, M. Colbert will be a great man if I raise him to the first rank.

I understand why he sought to destroy M. Fouquet.

He was envious.

Precisely, and his envy confined his wings.

He will henceforth be a winged serpent.

Despite the King's reconciliation, d'Artagnan felt some remains of hatred against his recent adversary.

Still, because the King commanded it, Colbert pressed the Musketeer's hand...

...and d'Artagnan was moved, and almost changed in his convictions.

D'Artagnan, you will go immediately and take possession of Belle-Isle-en-Mer.

Yes, sire.

Go, monsieur... and do not return without the keys of that place.

And so he had departed...

...with an injunction not to allow one inhabitant or refugee on Belle-Isle to escape...

...and with a command to blow up the fortress, in case of resistance.

BELLE-ISLE-EN-MER:

The sun had just gone down in the vast sheet of the reddened ocean, like a gigantic crucible...

We are lost, Porthos!

All fishing boats have fled the island, and none return--so we ourselves cannot depart.

But, Aramis... you told me that we are to hold Belle-Isle against the usurper...

So the lack of boats is not prejudicial to us in any way.

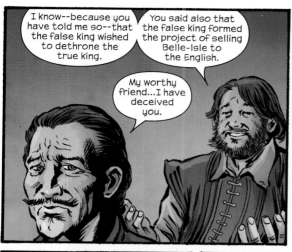

I know--because you have told me so--that the false king wished to dethrone the true king.

You said also that the false king formed the project of selling Belle-Isle to the English.

My worthy friend...I have deceived you.

I was serving not the King-- but the usurper, against whom Louis XIV, at this moment, is directing his efforts.

We are *rebels*, my poor friend.

The devil!

And--the duchy that was promised me--?

It was the usurper who was to give it to you.

"I called upon you, and you came to me, in remembrance of our ancient device...

"All for one, one for all!"

I have quite fallen out with Louis XIV...but I alone am the author of the plot.

Louis has no longer but the one enemy... myself alone.

I have made you a prisoner...so today I liberate you.

Fly back to your prince, Porthos.

You have been wrong in deceiving me, with that promised duchy.

But, seeing that you have acted entirely for yourself, it is impossible for me to blame you.

So now you see the real reason I have prepared cannon, muskets, and engines of all sorts.

But hark! I hear a hail for landing at the port.

It is d'Artagnan!

Your boats are all seized, my friends--and my officer spies upon me for M. Colbert and the King.

If you do not surrender to me, I am to fire upon the Isle within the hour, and then storm it.

We must remain at Belle-Isle.

I assure you, d'Artagnan, I will not surrender easily.

Let us say *adieu*, then.

But in truth, Porthos, *you* ought to go with him.

No. I will remain here.

Good-bye, old comrades.

And so d'Artagnan left Belle-Isle with the inseparable companion M. Colbert had given him.

But the captain of Musketeers had discovered an idea...

Monsieur, I shall go carry my resignation to the King.

You will do nothing until a new captain has taken my place.

Read this, M. d'Artagnan.

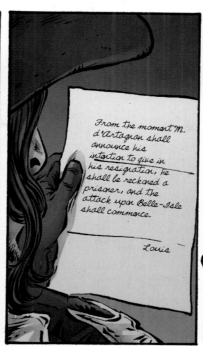

From the moment M. d'Artagnan shall announce his intention to give in his resignation, he shall be reckoned a prisoner, and the attack upon Belle-Isle shall commence.

Louis

Even as the boat touched the soil of France, the sound of a distant cannon rolled over the waters...

The fire is opened upon Belle-Isle, M. d'Artagnan.

BARROOOOM

As, upon the island...

I feel fatigued, Aramis... and have made out my will.

So my father did, when his legs failed him.

Mine are fine right now, but...

BARROOOOM

The fleet! The fleet's within half cannon-shot!

To arms!

Ay! To arms!

Both comrades rushed forth to their cannon batteries on the shore.

Boats, laden with soldiers, were seen approaching...from three directions.

They landed...

...and the combat commenced hand to hand.

What's the matter, Porthos?

Nothing! Only my legs.

It is really incomprehensible!

But they will be better when we charge!

In fact, Porthos and Aramis did animate their men with such vigor that the royalists soon re-embarked, without gaining anything but the wounds they carried away...

We must have a prisoner!

Quick!

Here is a prisoner for you.

Well! Have you not slandered your legs?

It was not with my legs I took him.

It was with my arms.

Knowing there would be a second assault, they interrogated their captive...

What did you contemplate doing with the leaders of Belle-Isle?

The orders are to kill during the combat, and hang afterwards.

I am too light for the gallows.

And I am too heavy.

People like me are not hung.

People like me break the cord.

I am sure that we could have procured you what sort of death you preferred.

I am George de Biscarrat. My father, one of Cardinal Richelieu's men, dueled with you when you served with the Muske--

BAOOOM

Cannon--and musketry!

This attack was but a feint, whilst their companions effected a landing on the far side of the island.

The terrified crowd rushes here-- demanding assistance and advice from us.

My friends-- M. Fouquet, your protector, has been thrown into the Bastille by an order of the King.

Avenge Monsieur Fouquet!

Death to the royalists!

No, my friends--no resistance.

Humble yourselves before God and the King.

Lay down your arms, as the King commands, and retire peaceably to your dwellings.

I command you to do so, in the name of M. Fouquet.

M. de Biscarrat, be kind enough to resume your liberty.

You will perhaps obtain some grace for us by informing the King's lieutenant on the manner in which submission has been effected.

I will go, messieurs.

We must repair to the grotto of Locmaria, Porthos.

Our boat awaits us...and the King has not caught us yet!

Midnight had struck as they reached the deep grottos where the foreseeing Bishop of Vannes had made certain preparations...

Are you there, Yves?

Yes, monseigneur...

...with Goenne and his son.

That is well, my Bretons. Let us visit the barque.

Do not go too near with the light...

For, as you desired me, monseigneur, I have placed in a coffer, under the bench of the poop...

...the barrel of powder and the musket charges that you sent me from the fort.

Very well.

HAROOOOO

Barking dogs!

M. de Biscarrat has led the King's guards here.

We must kill the dogs as they pass this narrow opening.

When the near-score of men without hear no more of the dogs' baying...

It looks as dark as a wolf's mouth inside.

We might break our necks in it.

The crowd of young soldiers, however, rushed into the cave...

BLAMM

BLAMM BLAMM BLAMM

The discharge of musketry, growling like thunder, exploded within the natural vault...

...and the little troop reappeared--some pale, some bleeding--from the depths of the cavern.

What sort of people *are* those inside?

Do you remember the history of the bastion Saint-Gervais, Captain?

Yes...where four Musketeers held out against an army.

Well, the two men inside-- Aramis and Porthos-- were of those Musketeers...

...and it is *they* who held Belle-Isle for M. Fouquet.

A murmur ran through the ranks...for the names of those four Musketeers were venerated, as, in antiquity, the names of Hercules and Theseus.

Captain, I beg to be allowed to march at the head of the first platoon.

Keep your sword ready.

I shall not draw my sword against these men who freed me.

I do not go to kill.

I go to *be* killed.

Within the grotto of Locmaria...

We must fly!

But-- that stone ahead walls up the outlet...

I will see to it.

HNNNGGH

HRRRRRHH

SPLUNSSH

Daylight.

Prepare for an assault!

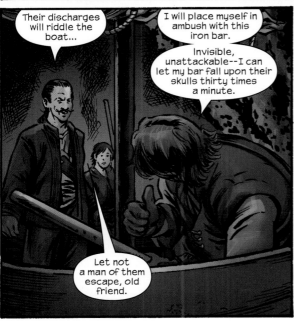

Their discharges will riddle the boat...

I will place myself in ambush with this iron bar.

Invisible, unattackable--I can let my bar fall upon their skulls thirty times a minute.

Let not a man of them escape, old friend.

Then came the sepulchral voice of Aramis...

STRIKE, PORTHOS!

THRUD

FTHUNK

Biscarrat was dead before he had ended his cry.

The formidable lever rose ten times in ten seconds...

...and made ten corpses.

URRGGGK

We walk in blood!

What caused this frightful carnage?

Fire! FIRE!

Come, Porthos.

When the two men have reached the last but one chamber in the cavern...

My friend, you will take this barrel of gunpowder--

--the match of which I am going to set fire to--

Do you understand me?

When a thing is explained to me, I understand it.

--and throw it amidst our enemies.

Then hasten to us.

Parbleu! Light it!

Begone, and give *me* the light.

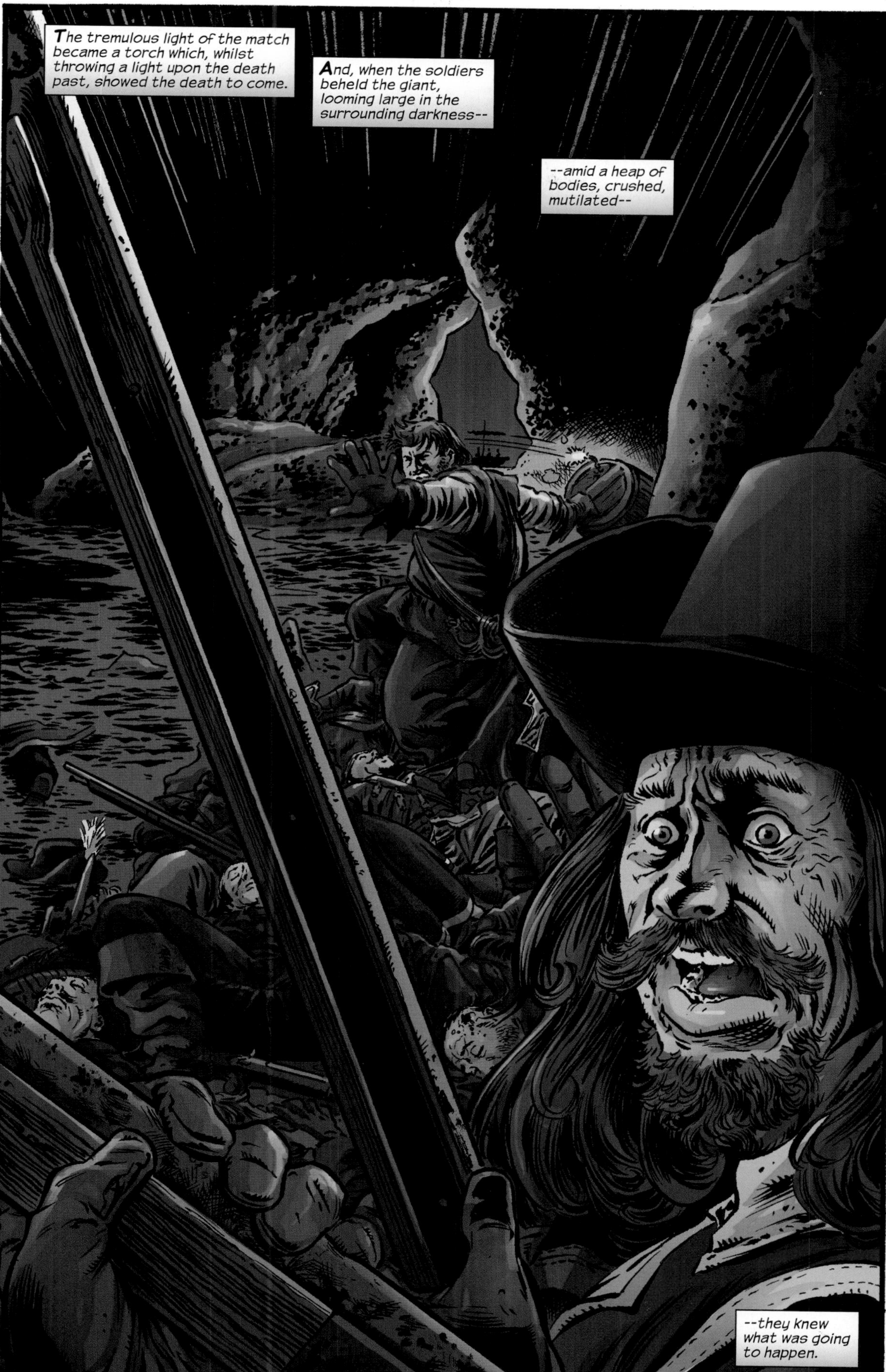
The tremulous light of the match became a torch which, whilst throwing a light upon the death past, showed the death to come.
And, when the soldiers beheld the giant, looming large in the surrounding darkness--
--amid a heap of bodies, crushed, mutilated--
--they knew what was going to happen.

Some endeavored to fly, but encountered the third brigade.

Others fired their muskets...

Others fell to their knees.

Liberty! Liberty for you if you will spare our lives!

UNNNHH

If I can tear out the match--

I am coming, my friends!

IN THE NAME OF HEAVEN, PORTHOS-- MAKE HASTE!

Oh! There is my *fatigue* seizing me again!

I can walk no farther!

What is this?

The shock of the explosion seemed to restore to Porthos the strength he had lost...

And he extended his vast hands to the right and left to repulse the falling rocks...

WATCH OUT, PORTHOS!

ARRRRHH

But a third granite mass sank between his two shoulders...

For an instant, the "Hercules of France" pushed back the lateral rocks, and seemed like the ancient angel of chaos.

...and he was swallowed up in a sepulchre of broken stones.

PORTHOS!

But then the monolith above brought the giant down upon his knees...

Raise up these rocks, Bretons!

Raise them up, I say!

Too...

...heavyyyy

And then the Titan sank quite down, breathing his last sigh.

Aramis listened, his breast oppressed, his heart ready to break.

Nothing more!

The giant slept the eternal sleep, in the tomb which God had made to his measure.

Though the Bretons carried Aramis to the barque, something of the dead Porthos had just died within him, as well.

Worthy Porthos! Even when dying, he had thought only that he was carrying out the conditions of his compact with Aramis.

And so the barque hoisted its sail...

...and made way with its head towards Spain, across the terrible Gulf of Gascony, so rife with tempests.

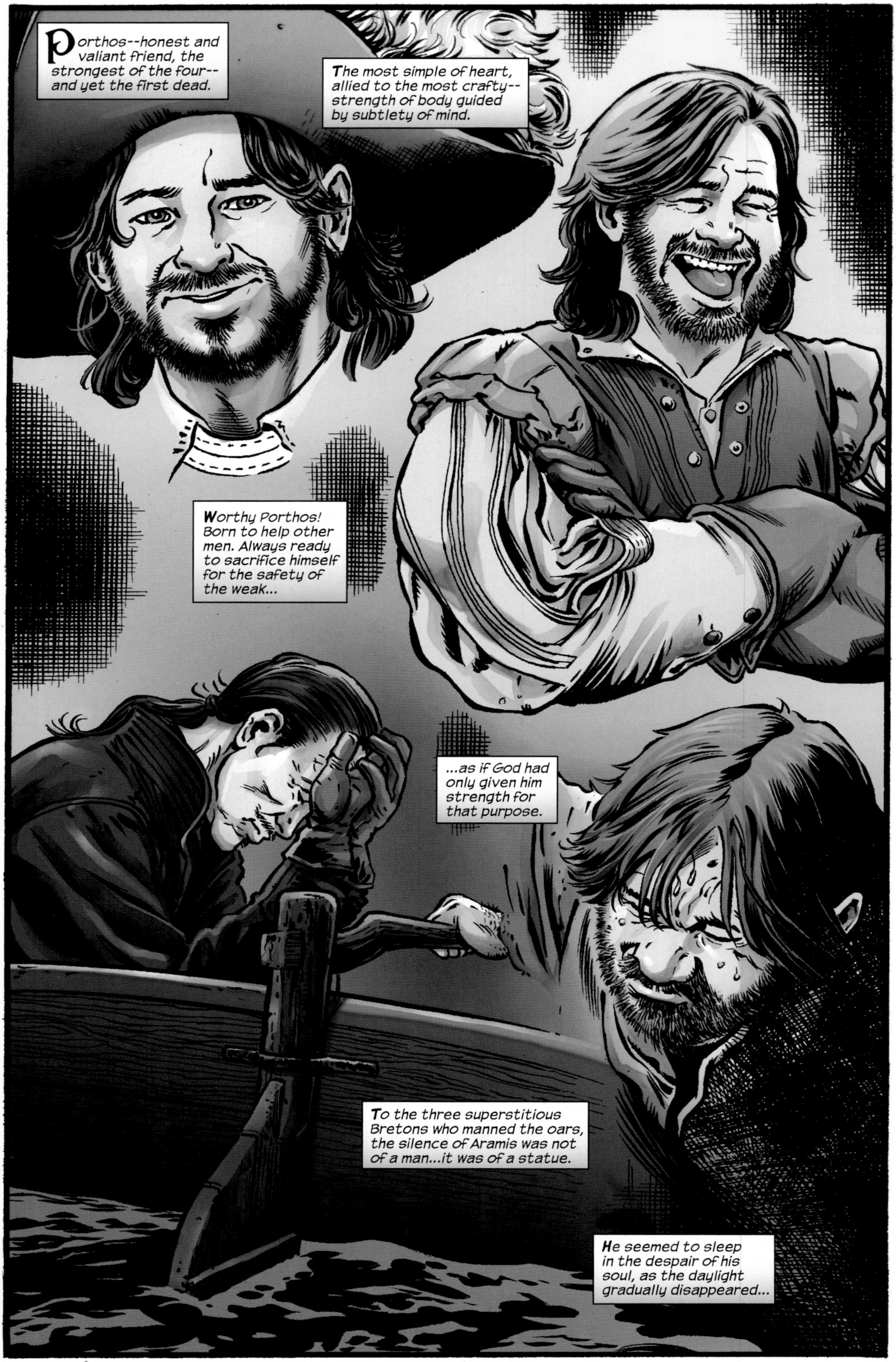
Porthos--honest and valiant friend, the strongest of the four--and yet the first dead.
The most simple of heart, allied to the most crafty--strength of body guided by subtlety of mind.
Worthy Porthos! Born to help other men. Always ready to sacrifice himself for the safety of the weak...
...as if God had only given him strength for that purpose.
To the three superstitious Bretons who manned the oars, the silence of Aramis was not of a man...it was of a statue.
He seemed to sleep in the despair of his soul, as the daylight gradually disappeared...

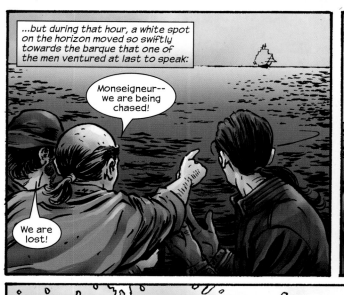

...but during that hour, a white spot on the horizon moved so swiftly towards the barque that one of the men ventured at last to speak:

Monseigneur-- we are being chased!

We are lost!

At length, Aramis took a telescope from the bottom of the boat...

Here... look!

Don't be alarmed. If there is any sin in such an instrument, I will take it upon myself.

Miséricorde!

They are firing at us!

BAOOM

SPLISSSH

Give us your orders, monseigneur. We are ready to die for you.

Let us wait.

If we endeavor to fly, they will sink us.

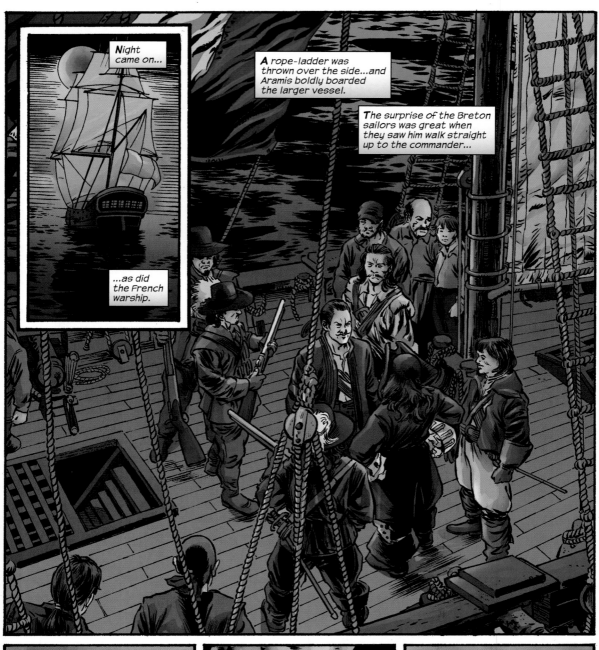

Night came on...

...as did the French warship.

A rope-ladder was thrown over the side...and Aramis boldly boarded the larger vessel.

The surprise of the Breton sailors was great when they saw him walk straight up to the commander...

...and make a mysterious sign to him.

Five minutes later, Aramis emerged with the captain from his cabin...

Point the head of the ship toward Corunna*...

*A Spanish port.

That night saw Aramis leaning upon the bulwarks...

...and witnessed, perhaps, the first tears had ever fallen from his eyes.

D'Artagnan, trembling with rage, had gone straight to the castle at Nantes and sent the King word of his resignation as Captain of the Musketeers.

It was accepted.

At last, he was ushered into the King's apartment...

I am here, sire.

Monsieur... what did I charge you to go and do at Belle-Isle? Tell me, if you please.

It is not of me that questions should be asked, sire...

...but of that infinite number of officers to whom were given an infinite number of orders.

Monsieur, orders have only been given to such as were judged faithful.

And therefore, I have been astonished, sire, that a captain like myself, who ranks with the marshals of France...

...should have found himself under the orders of five or six lieutenants or majors.

It was such insults, offered to a brave man, that led me to respectfully offer Your Majesty my resignation.

And I have accepted it, monsieur.

It was a cruelty on Your Majesty's part to send me to capture my friends and lead them to your gallows.

One would say you have forgotten what these men have done to me.

At this moment, my soldiers have taken Belle-Isle... and the rebels have fled.

Lofty heads have bowed to me, Monsieur d'Artagnan.

Bow yours... or choose the exile that will best suit you.

Are you content, sire?

Reckoning from today, I have no longer any enemies in France.

It remains with me to send you to a foreign field to gather your marshal's baton.*

Depend upon me for finding you an opportunity.

* To gain France's highest military office by winning victories abroad.

That is all kind and well!

But-- those poor men at Belle-Isle-- one, in particular, so good...so brave... so true!

Do you ask their pardon of me?

Upon my knees, sire.

Well! Then go and take it to them, if it be still time.

But do you answer for their behavior in the future?

With my life, sire!

And, with a heart swelling with joy, d'Artagnan rushed out of the castle, on his way to Belle-Isle.

But he would soon learn that Porthos was dead, and that Aramis had escaped to the territories of the King of Spain.

At his old friend's baronial estate, some days later, d'Artagnan listened to the reading of Porthos' will...

"...and, having no relations, I have left all my property to M. le Vicomte Raoul Auguste Jules de Bragelonne..."

Raoul--son of their mutual friend Athos, Count de la Fère.

Raoul--who has gone to Africa with the hope of dying in combat.

Athos, meanwhile, had become an old man in a week, upon receiving a letter from Aramis, in Spain...

Porthos is dead!

I dreamed last night that dear Raoul came to me, and told me as much.

Oh, Raoul-- Raoul! Thou keepest thy promise!

Thou warnest me!

Then Athos felt his head become confused... his legs give way...

His servants sent for a physician, who made two successive bleedings that left the patient very weak... yet his fever ceased at midnight.

The physician departed, declaring that the Count was saved.

Then commenced for Athos a strange, indefinable state...

Free to think, his mind turned towards his beloved son...

Raoul...

*H*is imagination painted the fields of Africa in the environs of Gigelli,* where the *Duke de Beaufort* must have landed his army and fought a battle.

*A*n inexpressible shudder of horror seized him to recognize the uniform of the soldiers of Picardy...

...saw all the gaping, cold wounds looking up to the azure heavens as if to demand back from them the souls to which they had opened a passage...

*Modern-day Sierra Leone.

...saw the body of M. de Beaufort, in the first ranks of the dead.

Then he saw a form appear...

Raoul.

The Count attempted to utter a cry...

But it remained stifled in his throat.

And as he gained the crest of the hill, he beheld his son rising into the void...

...departing toward heaven...

...when the charm was suddenly broken.

RAOUL....!

Athos did not stir as he heard a horse galloping through his gates...

He scarcely turned his head as a heavy step ascended the stairs...

He beheld his son's servant, who had accompanied him to Africa...

Grimaud...!

Yes, Monsieur le Comte.

Raoul is dead, is he not?

Yes.

HERE I AM!

Athos, my friend!...

Monsieur le Chevalier d'Artagnan!

Where is he?

Where...?

He died... when he learned of his son's death.

Adieu, old friend...

D'Artagnan arose, tearing himself from the chamber where he had just found dead...

...the one to whom he had come to report the news of the death of Porthos...

So heart-rending were his sobs that the Count's servants answered them with their own lamentable clamors.

At daybreak, Grimaud gave d'Artagnan a letter written by M. de Beaufort before he himself had died...

My Dear Count--

Amidst a great triumph, your son, M. de Bragelonne, has died gloriously.

After his death in battle, we discovered a lock of fair hair in his right hand...and that hand was pressed tightly upon his heart.

Your good friend,

Le Duc de Beaufort

Oh, unhappy boy! A suicide!

But they have kept their words to each other-- and are now reunited.

On the morrow, the cold remains of both father and son--whose body had been embalmed that he might be buried in France--were returned to the earth...

I shall follow thy funerals, my friends-- I, already old--I, who am of no value on earth...

And I shall scatter dust upon those brows.

Left alone at last to bid a last adieu to the double grave which contained his two lost friends, d'Artagnan forgot the hour, while thinking of the dead...

And he heard a woman praying...and weeping.

≶Sobbb...≷

Mademoiselle de la Vallière! You--*here*?

M. d'Artagnan...

I should better have liked to see you decked with flowers in the mansion of the Comte de la Fère!

You would have wept less-- I, too!

I know I have caused the death of the Vicomte de Bragelonne...and thereby, his father.

But... I must go. The King's carriage awaits.

You see, madam, that your happiness still lasts.

A day will come, monsieur, when you will repent of having so ill-judged me.

For Raoul, I would have given my *life* without hesitation...

But I could not give my *love.*

FOUR YEARS LATER:

M. Fouquet cannot comprehend that banishment is liberty, falconer...

...any more than I can get used to being called a *"Count,"* even after four years.

Is M. Fouquet well, Monsieur le Comte?

He had a near chance of the scaffold, before the King merely banished him.

I left the court mourning the death of the Queen-Mother...

And Louise de Vallière was right...

I *do* feel pity for her, now that she has been replaced by another in the King's affections.

M. Colbert approaches, monsieur...

Good day, M. d'Artagnan. Have you had a pleasant journey?

Yes, monsieur.

The King wishes to invite you to his table for this evening.

You will meet an old friend there...

...M. le Duc d'Almĕda, who is arrived this morning from Spain.

A Spanish duke--an old friend of mine?

I!

Perhaps *now* you will recognize me...

Aramis!

So you, the exile, are again in France!

And I shall dine with you at the King's table.

M. Colbert, as minister of finance, was kind enough to arrange it.

It was my pleasure, Monsieur le Duc.

He counts upon my influence to keep Spain neutral in the coming war with the United Provinces.*

*The Netherlands.

King Louis' favorite new game is war.

His greed has expanded beyond the boundaries of France.

He even wants to ally with the English King Charles, so he can have the support of the English Navy in a war against the Dutch.

It is a war which, otherwise, the French would be ill-prepared to fight.

It is all very well to make sure France has ships--but it will still need a fine army, finely led...

...or else, in the Dutch lands, soldiers will be drowned for want of a boat, a plank, or a stick.

But then, it is my profession to die for His Majesty.

I never heard of an instance of a marshal of France being drowned, d'Artagnan.

I--a marshal of France?

A man must have commanded an expedition in chief to obtain the baton.

I have brought you a plan of a campaign you will lead a body of troops to carry out in the next spring.

I implore you to tell the King that he may depend upon a victory, or seeing me dead.

Then I will have the fleur-de-lis for your marshal's baton prepared immediately.

And you will, perhaps, never see me again, dear d'Artagnan.

I am old...

I am extinguished...

I am dead.

My friend, you will live longer than I shall.

Diplomacy commands you to live...but for my part, honor condemns me to die.

Bah! Such men as we are, Monsieur le Marshal, only die satiated with joy or glory.

I assure you, Monsieur le Duc, I feel very little appetite for either.

Let us love each other for four...

...though we are now but two.

Two hours later, they were separated.

Soon, with Spain neutral, the English Navy, ballasted by a few millions of French gold, made a devastating campaign against the Dutch fleets.

In the spring, M. d'Artagnan's army of 12,000 men took twelve places in northern Holland within a month...

...and he was in the fifth day of a siege against the thirteenth.

The reconstruction of the trenches is complete, M. d'Artagnan.

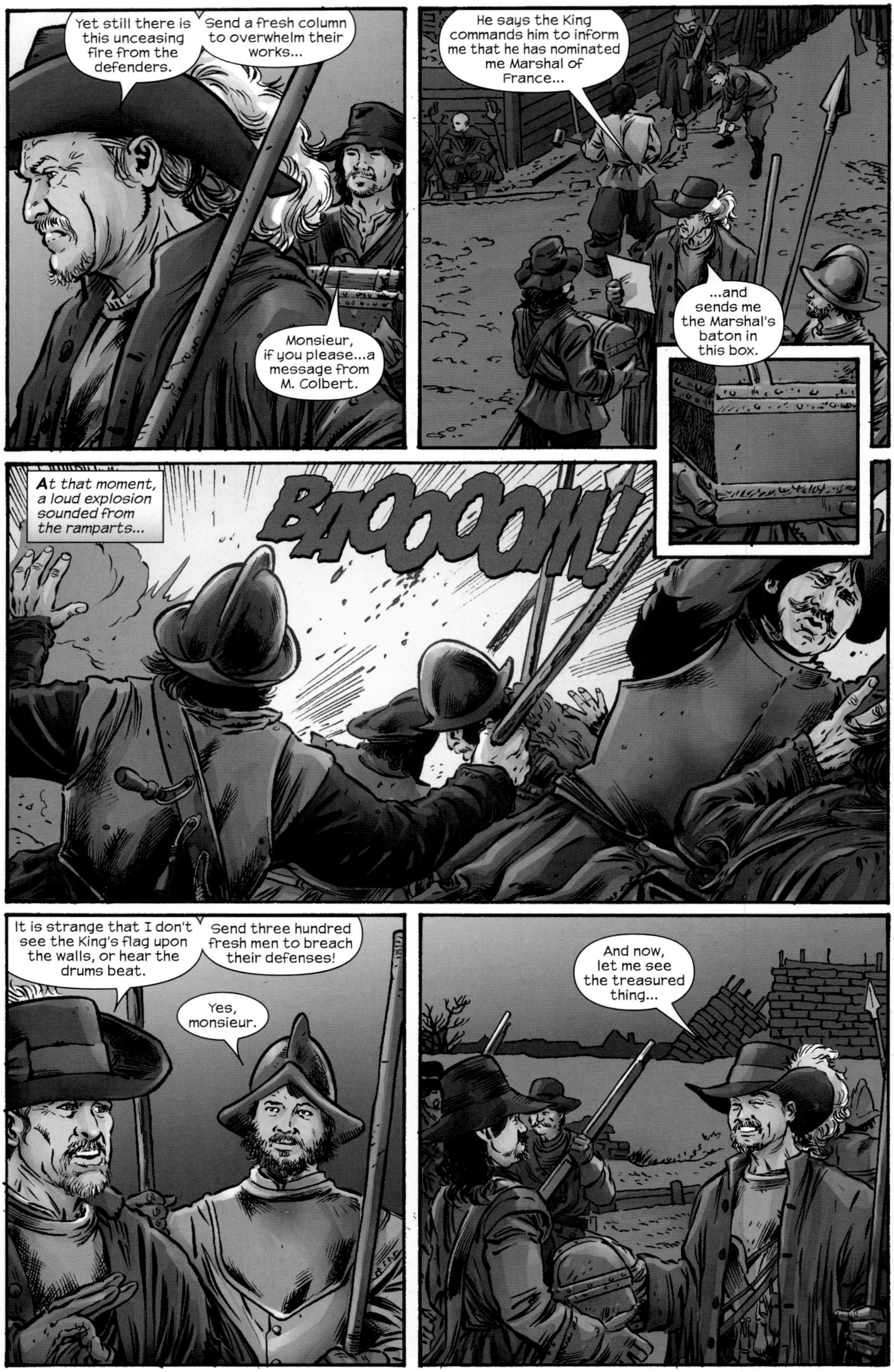
Yet still there is this unceasing fire from the defenders.
Send a fresh column to overwhelm their works...
Monsieur, if you please...a message from M. Colbert.
He says the King commands him to inform me that he has nominated me Marshal of France...
...and sends me the Marshal's baton in this box.
At that moment, a loud explosion sounded from the ramparts...
BADOOOOM!
It is strange that I don't see the King's flag upon the walls, or hear the drums beat.
Send three hundred fresh men to breach their defenses!
Yes, monsieur.
And now, let me see the treasured thing...

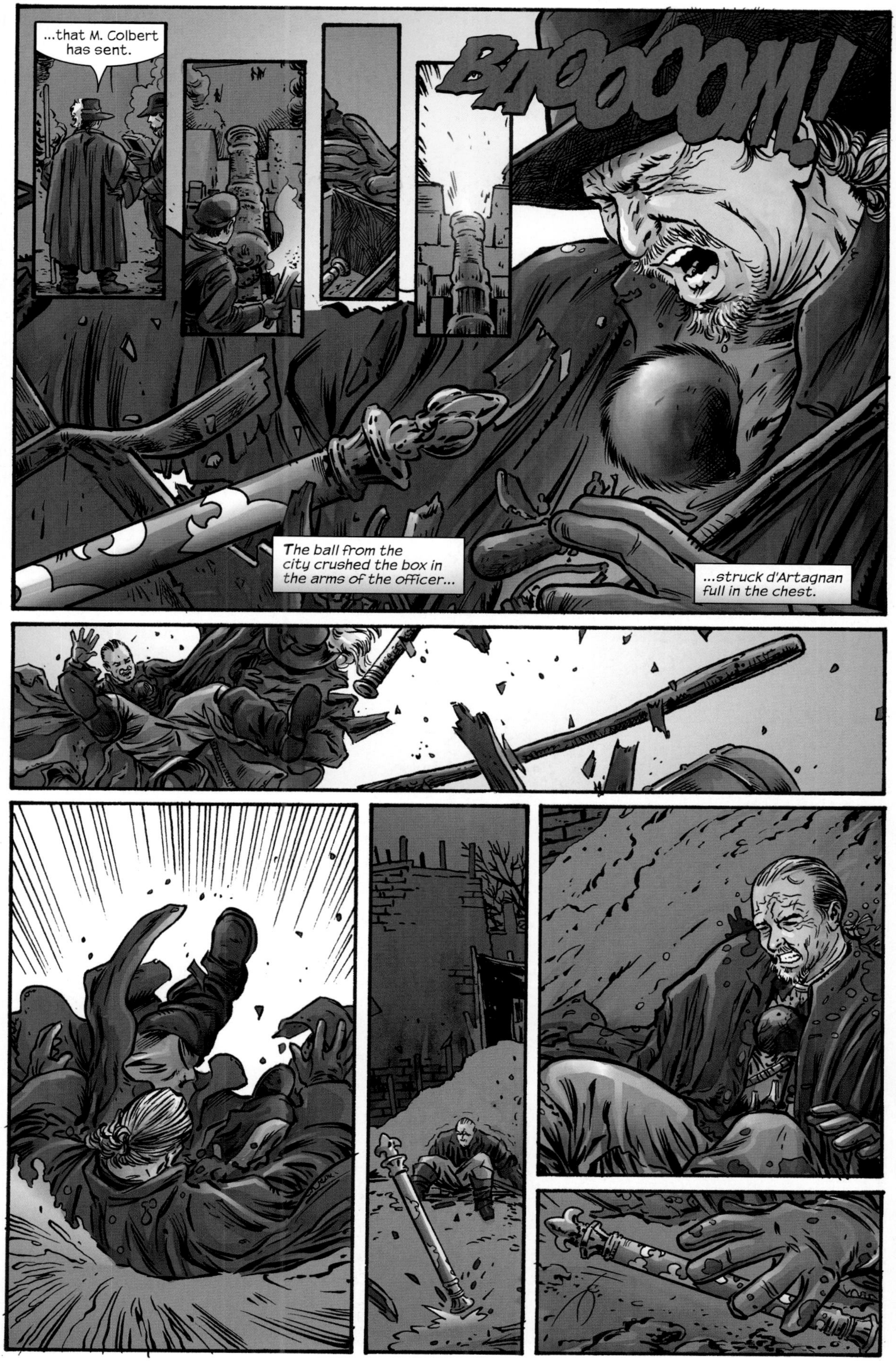
...that M. Colbert has sent.
BROOOOM!
The ball from the city crushed the box in the arms of the officer...
...struck d'Artagnan full in the chest.

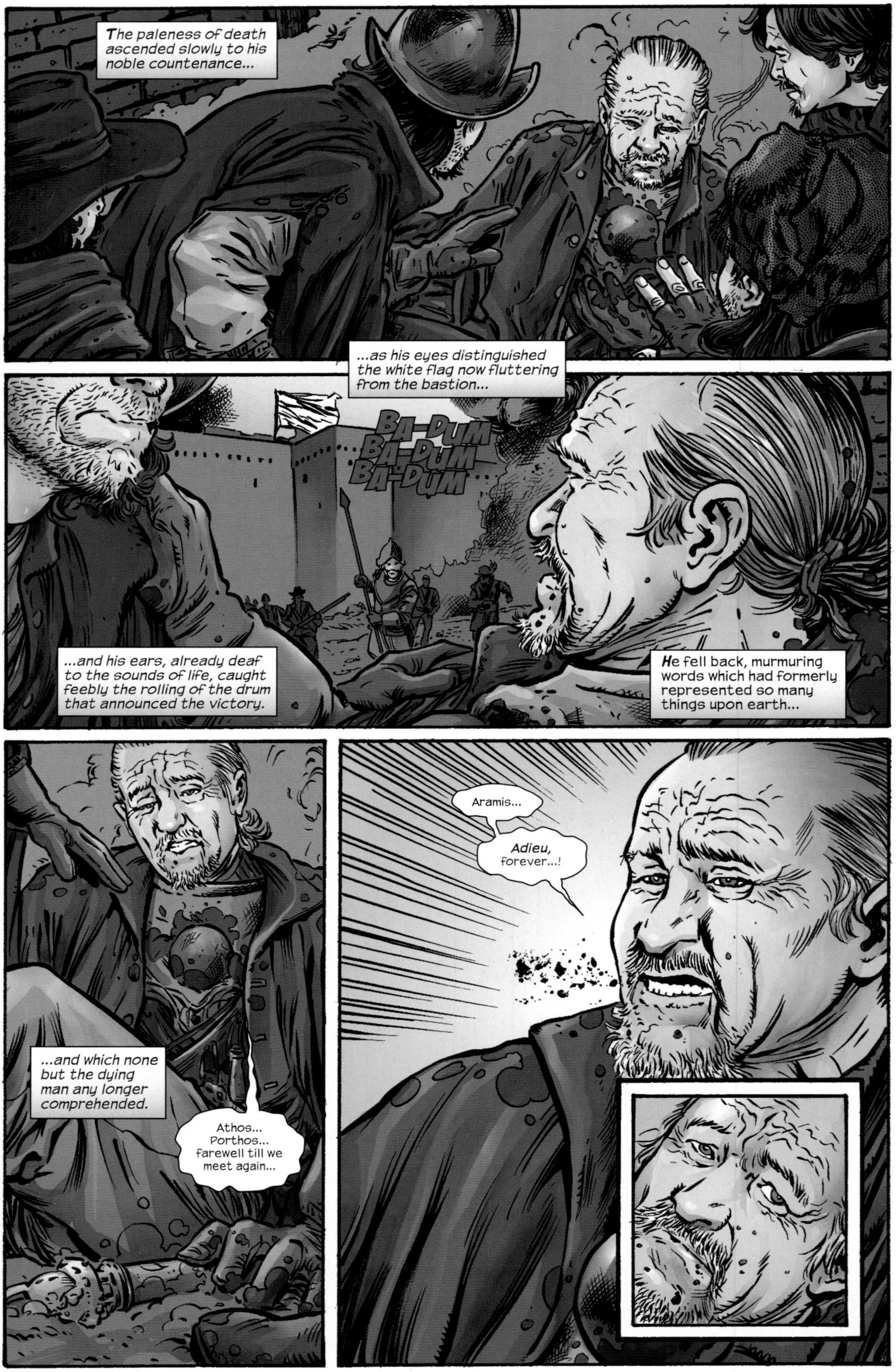
The paleness of death ascended slowly to his noble countenance...
...as his eyes distinguished the white flag now fluttering from the bastion...
BA-DUM BA-DUM BA-DUM
...and his ears, already deaf to the sounds of life, caught feebly the rolling of the drum that announced the victory.
He fell back, murmuring words which had formerly represented so many things upon earth...
...and which none but the dying man any longer comprehended.
Athos... Porthos... farewell till we meet again...
Aramis...
Adieu, forever...!

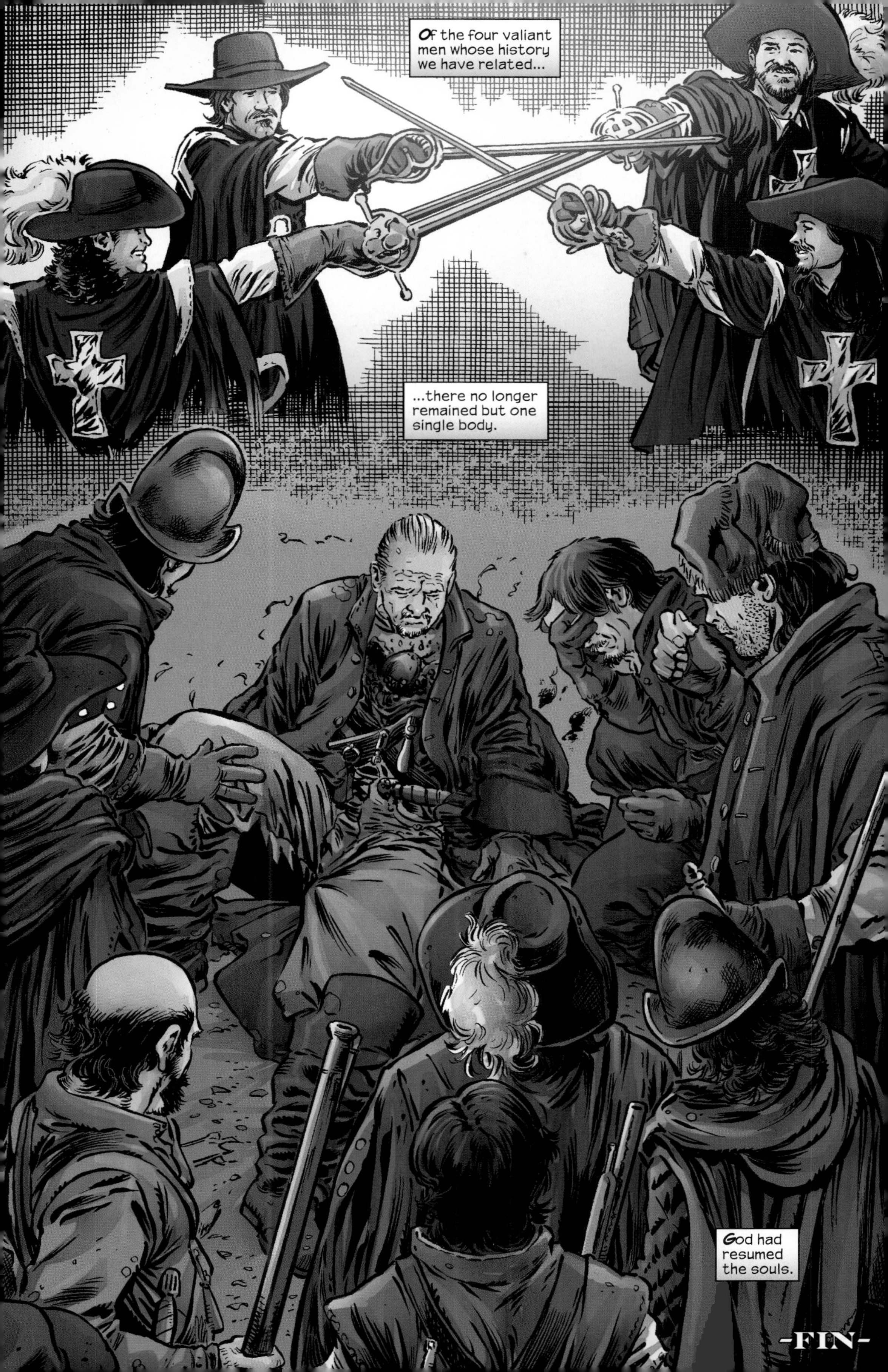
Of the four valiant men whose history we have related...
...there no longer remained but one single body.
God had resumed the souls.
-FIN-

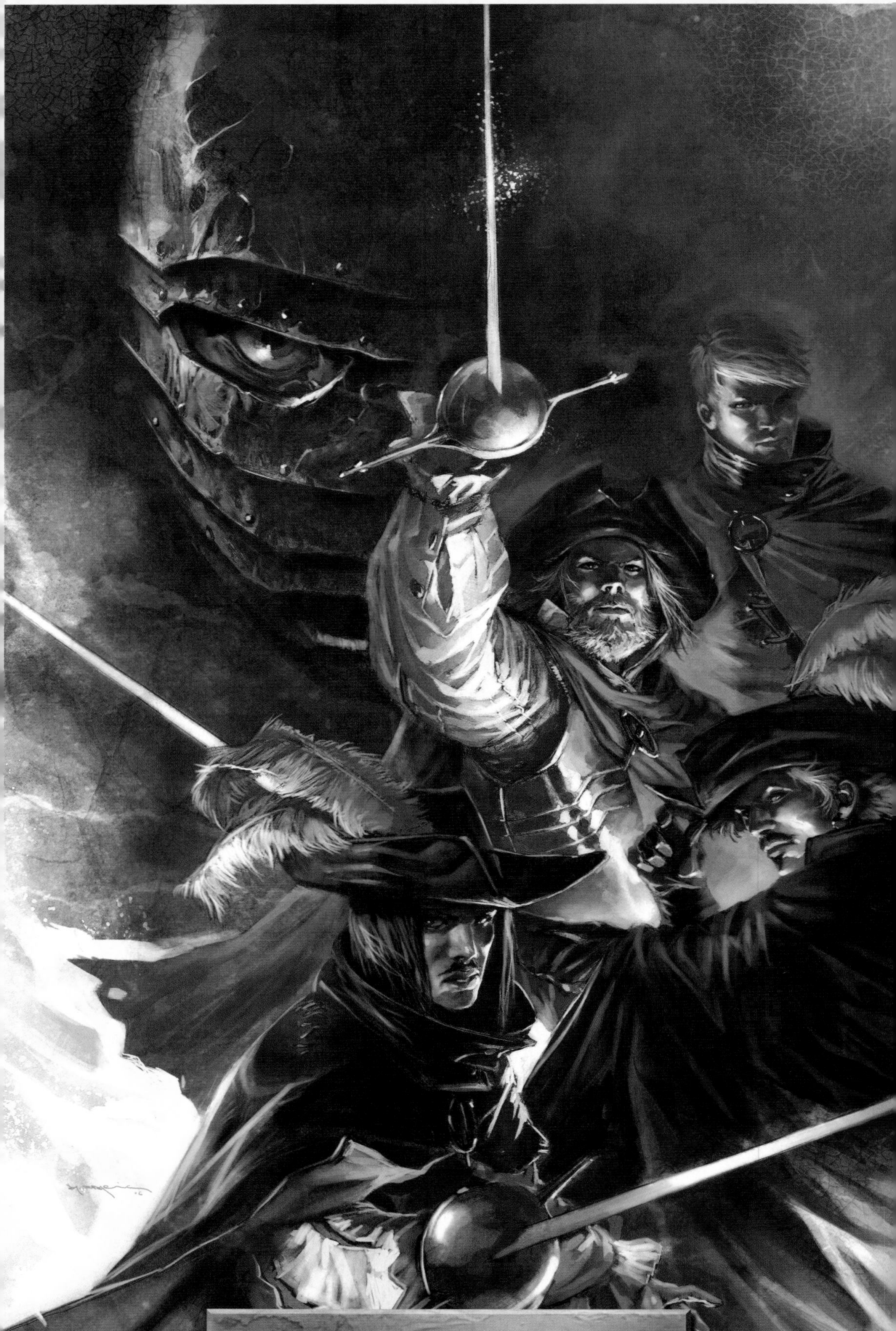

COVER #1

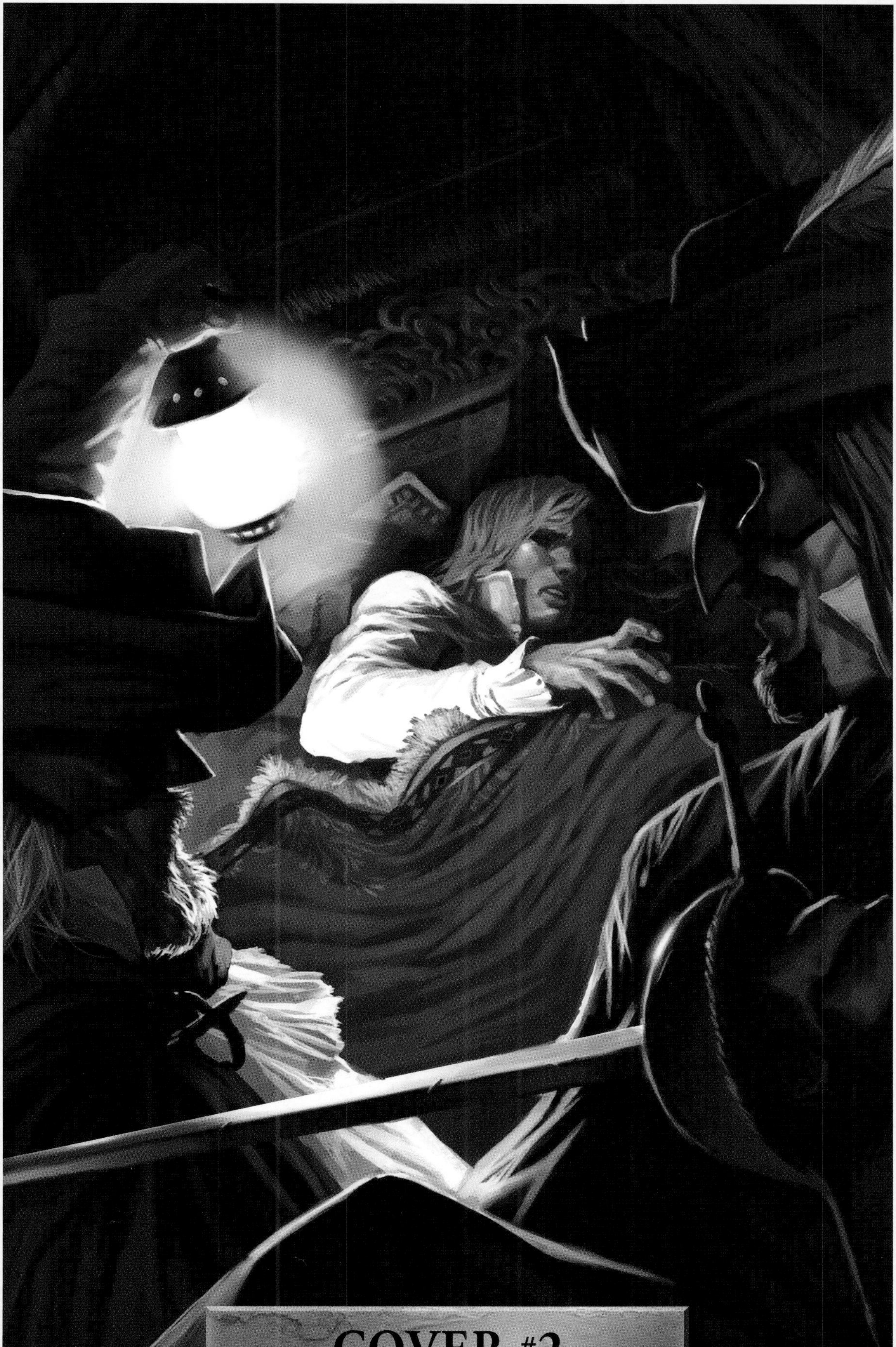

COVER #2

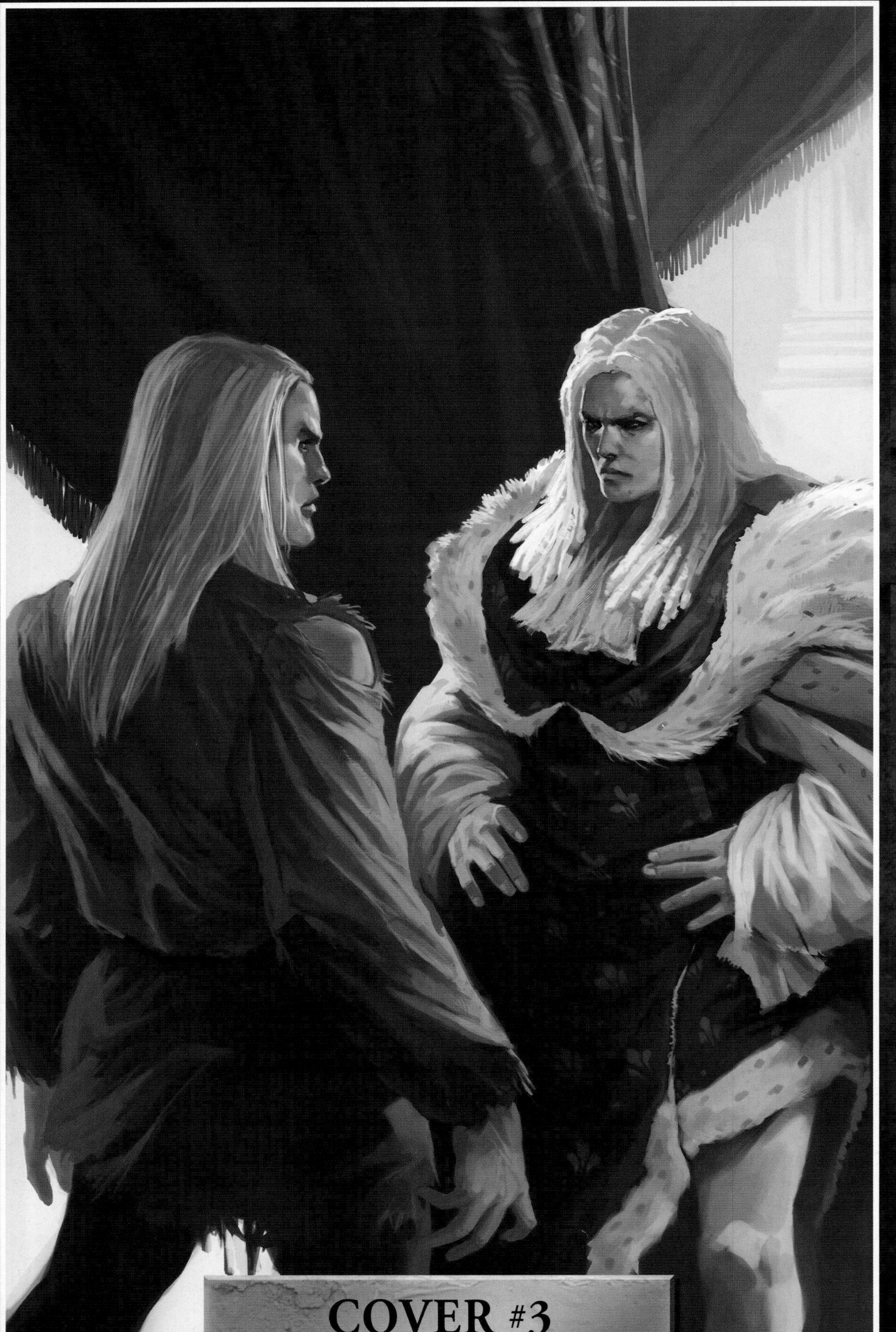

COVER #3

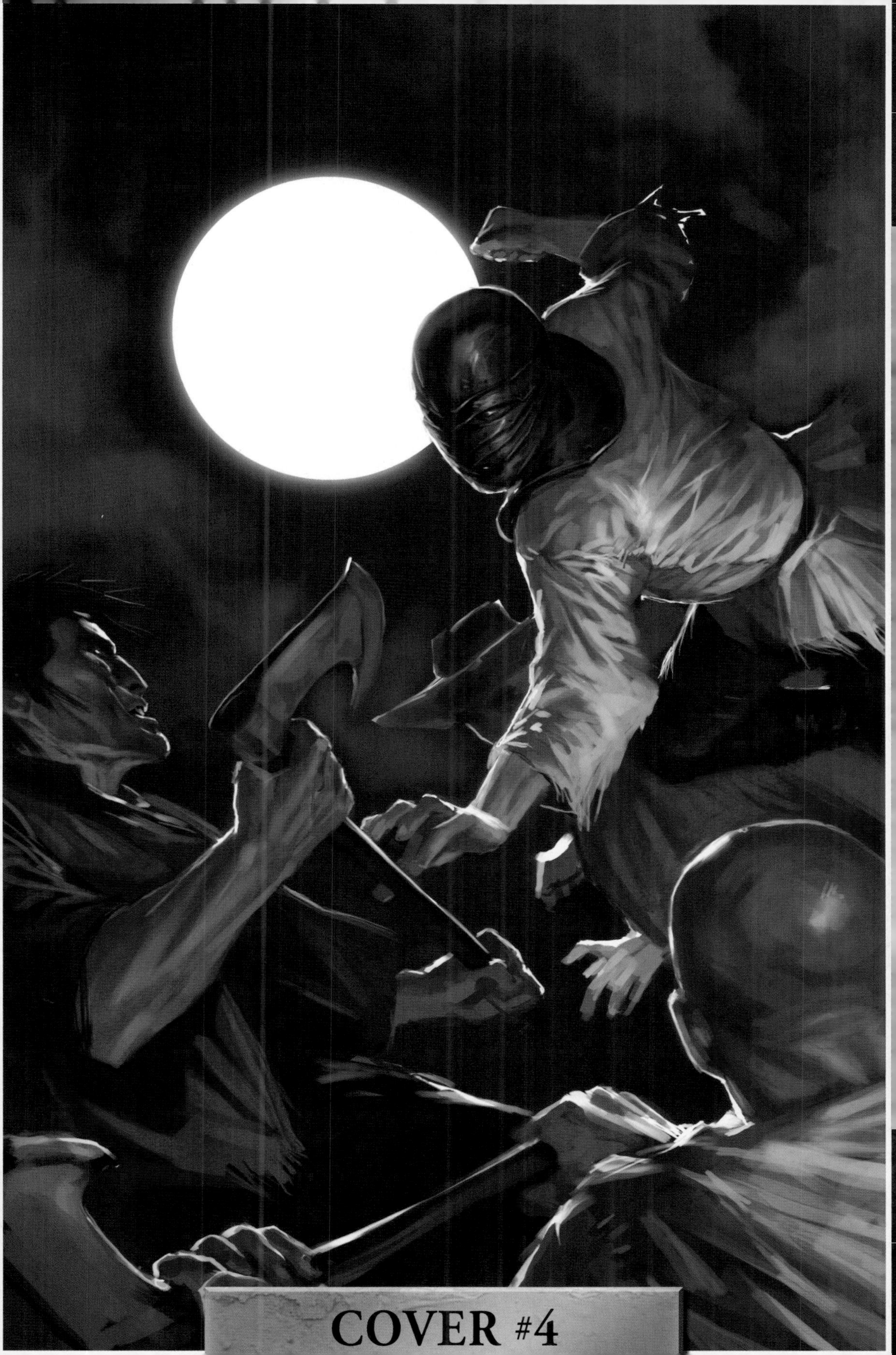

COVER #4

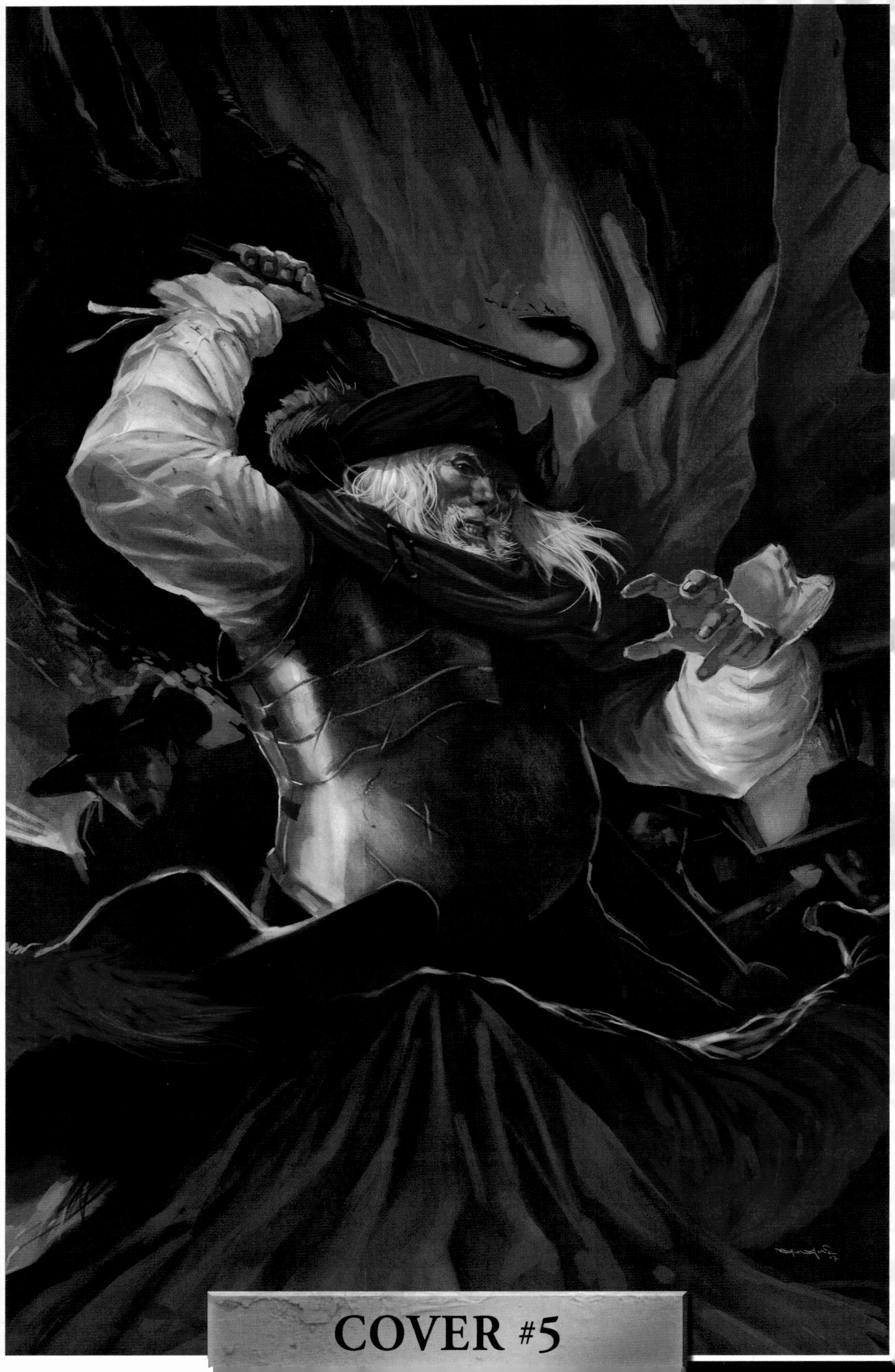

COVER #5

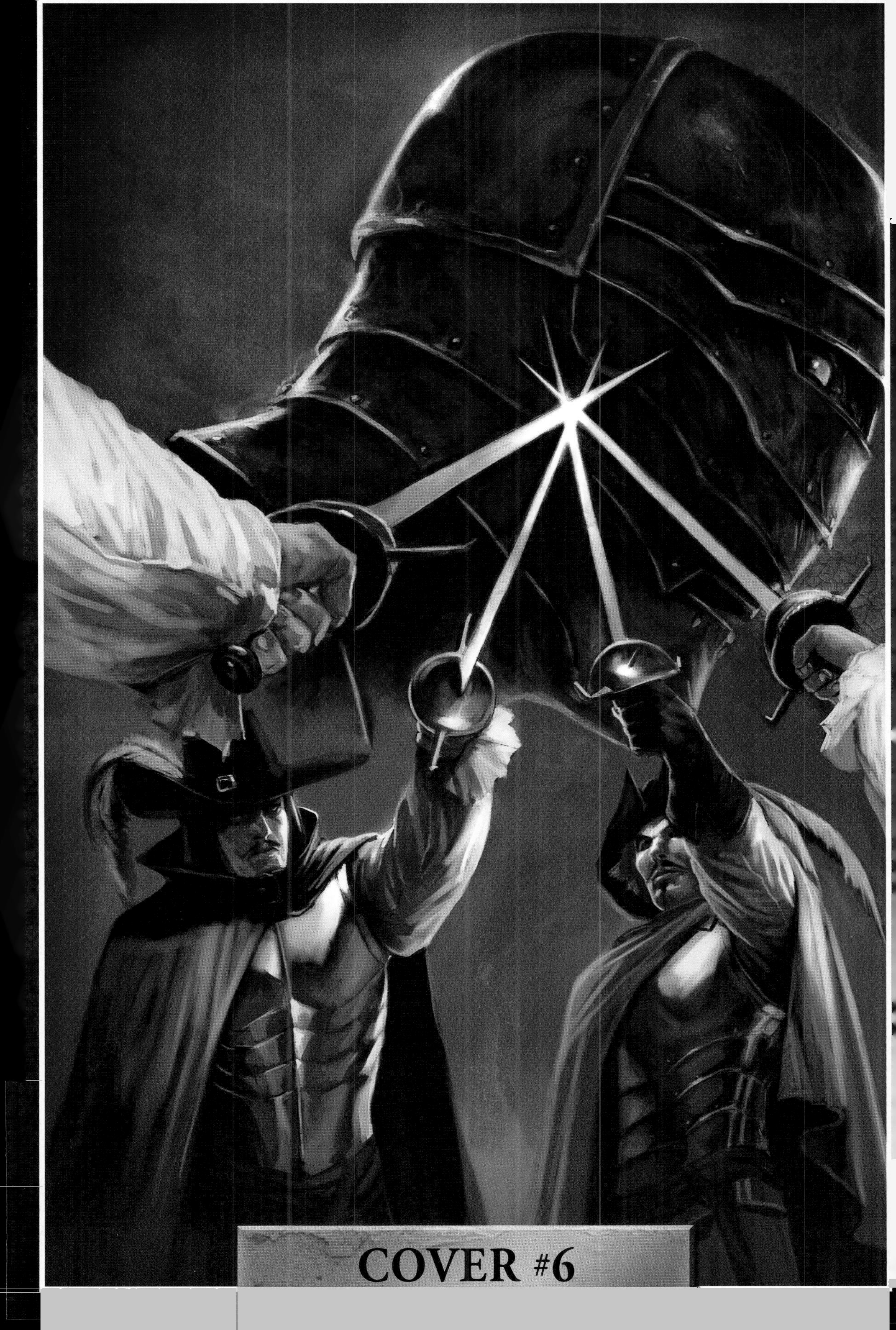

COVER #6

The Man in the Iron Mask
Glossary

Antiquity - the quality of being ancient

Azure - of or having a light, purplish shade of blue

Bade - to command; order

Barque - a small vessel that is propelled by oars or sails

Bastille - a fortress in Paris, used as a prison, built in the 14th century
and destroyed July 14, 1789

Battery - two or more pieces of artillery used for combined action

Beset - to attack on all sides

Bleeding – outdated medical procedure of draining large amounts of blood
in hopes of curing afflictions

Bulwark - a wall of earth or other material built for defense

Cavalier - a man escorting a woman or acting
as her partner in dancing

Chastise - to criticize severely

Château - a castle or fortress

Confer - to consult together

Confessor - a priest authorized to hear confessions

Consummating – to fulfill

Corps - a group of persons associated or
acting together

Countenance - the face; visage

Earnestness - serious in intention, purpose, or effort

Effrontery - shameless or impudent boldness

Fête - a festive celebration or entertainment

Impregnable - strong enough to resist or withstand attack

Injunction - order requiring someone to refrain from doing a particular act

Luminous - radiating or reflecting light

Midwife - a person trained to assist women in childbirth

Monseigneur - a French title of honor given to princes, bishops, and other persons of eminence

Poniard - a dagger typically having a slender square or triangular blade

Presage - something that foreshadows a future event

Procure - to obtain or get with care

Promenade - an area used for walking

Reposing - the state of being at rest

Sepulchral - serving as a tomb

Sheathe - to enclose in a casing or covering

Sowing - to propagate; disseminate

Squander - to spend wastefully or extravagantly

Stouter - bulky in figure

Tempest - violent windstorm, frequently accompanied by rain, snow, or hail

Theorbos - an obsolete bass lute

Venerate - to regard or treat with reverence

Alexandre Dumas
(1802-1870)

The son of a general in Napoleon's army, the acclaimed French writer Alexandre Dumas is credited with reviving the historical novel in France thanks to his most popular works, including *The Three Musketeers*, *The Man in the Iron Mask*, and the *Count of Monte Cristo*.

Born in Villes-Cotterêts, France, Dumas worked as a notary early in his life. Eventually, thanks to his elegant handwriting, Dumas became the notary of King Louis Philippe himself. Later on, Dumas became a magazine publisher for a local theatre.

In 1829, Dumas made his mark, first as a playwright, with the play "*Henri III et Sa Cour.*" Its success led to several more plays penned by Dumas. His play "*La Tour de Nesle*" is regarded by many to be one of the greatest French melodramas in French history.

His success on the stage opened the doors for Dumas to rejuvenate the genre of French historical novels, which is where he made most of his fortune. With the help of over 70 assistants, Dumas wrote over 250 books.

Alexandre Dumas' Must-Reads

Ali Pacha	*The Count of Monte Cristo*
Chicot the Jester	*The Forty-Five Guardsmen*
Louise de la Valliere	*The Man in the Iron Mask*
Ten Years Later	*The Three Musketeers*
The Black Tulip	*The Vicomte de Bragelonne*
The Companions of Jehu	*Twenty Years After*

LEGENDARY TALES BROUGHT TO LIFE

The greatest stories of all time, written by the authors who forged history and drawn by masters of their craft for today's audience!

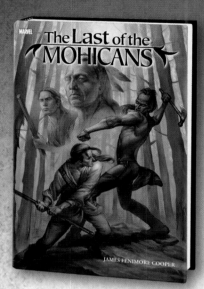

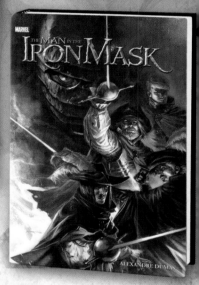

**MARVEL ILLUSTRATED:
THE LAST OF THE MOHICANS
HARDCOVER**
by James Fenimore Cooper
Rating: 15+
$19.99
ISBN: 978-0-7851-2443-6

**MARVEL ILLUSTRATED:
TREASURE ISLAND
HARDCOVER**
by Robert Louis Stevenson
Rating: 13+
$19.99
ISBN: 978-0-7851-2594-5

**MARVEL ILLUSTRATED:
THE MAN IN THE IRON MASK
HARDCOVER**
by Alexandre Dumas
Rating: 13+
$19.99
ISBN: 978-0-7851-2592-1

MARVEL ILLUSTRATED
Putting the "novel" back in Graphic Novel

ON SALE NOW
For a comic store near you, call 1-888-comicbook.

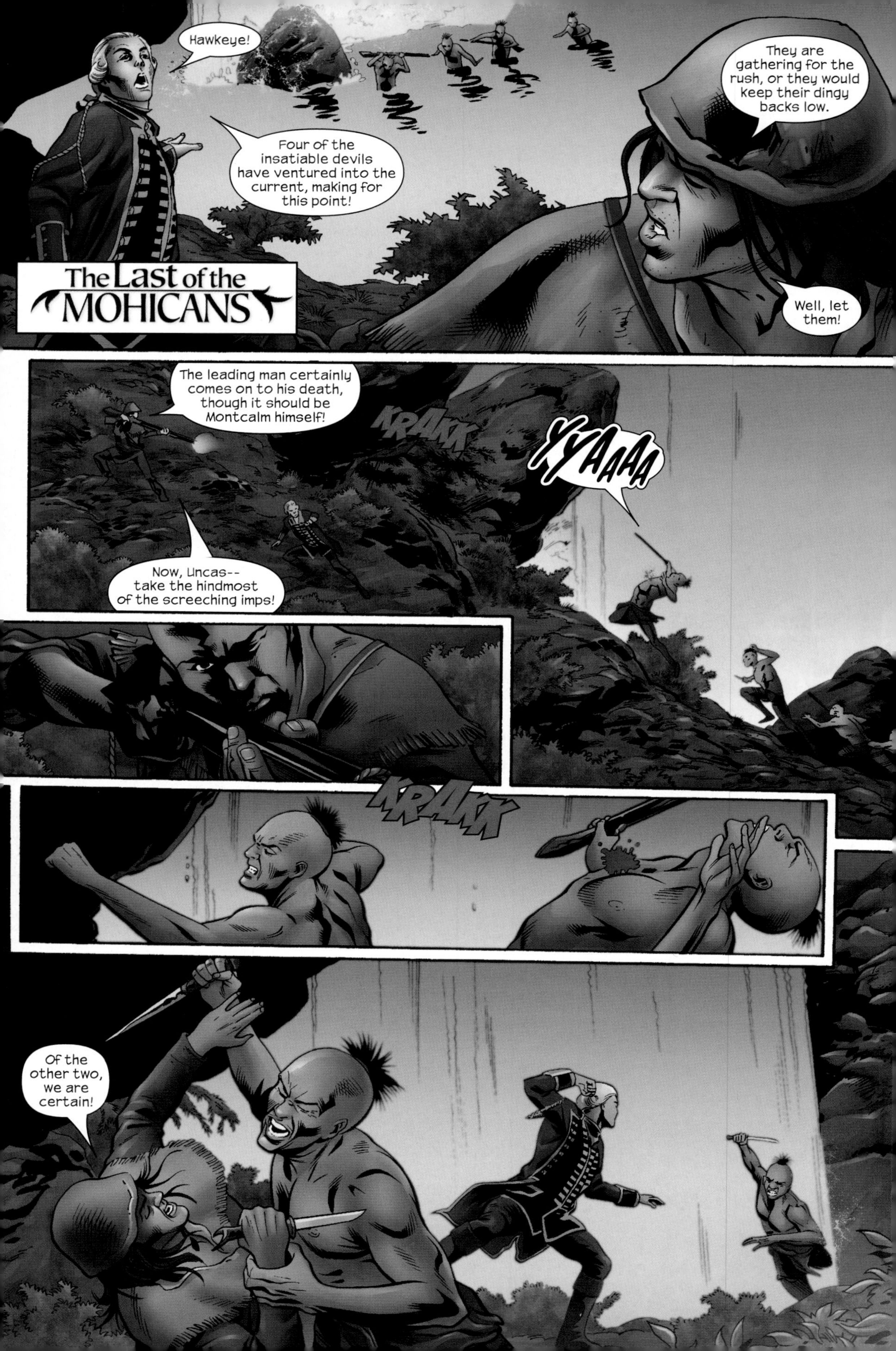

Hawkeye!
Four of the insatiable devils have ventured into the current, making for this point!
They are gathering for the rush, or they would keep their dingy backs low.
Well, let them!
The Last of the MOHICANS
The leading man certainly comes on to his death, though it should be Montcalm himself!
KRAKK
YYAAAAA
Now, Uncas-- take the hindmost of the screeching imps!
KRAKK
Of the other two, we are certain!

Come on...ye bloody-minded hell-hounds...

Ye meet a man--

--without a cross!*

HGGNNHH...

*One with no "Indian blood" in his veins.

Meanwhile, on the brink of the precipice, Heyward felt his foe's grasp at his throat...

...saw the savage's grim, triumphant smile.

Then--a dark hand...

A glancing knife...

Blood flowing from the severed tendons of his wrist...

...and the Mingo fell, fierce and disappointed, down the irrecoverable chasm.

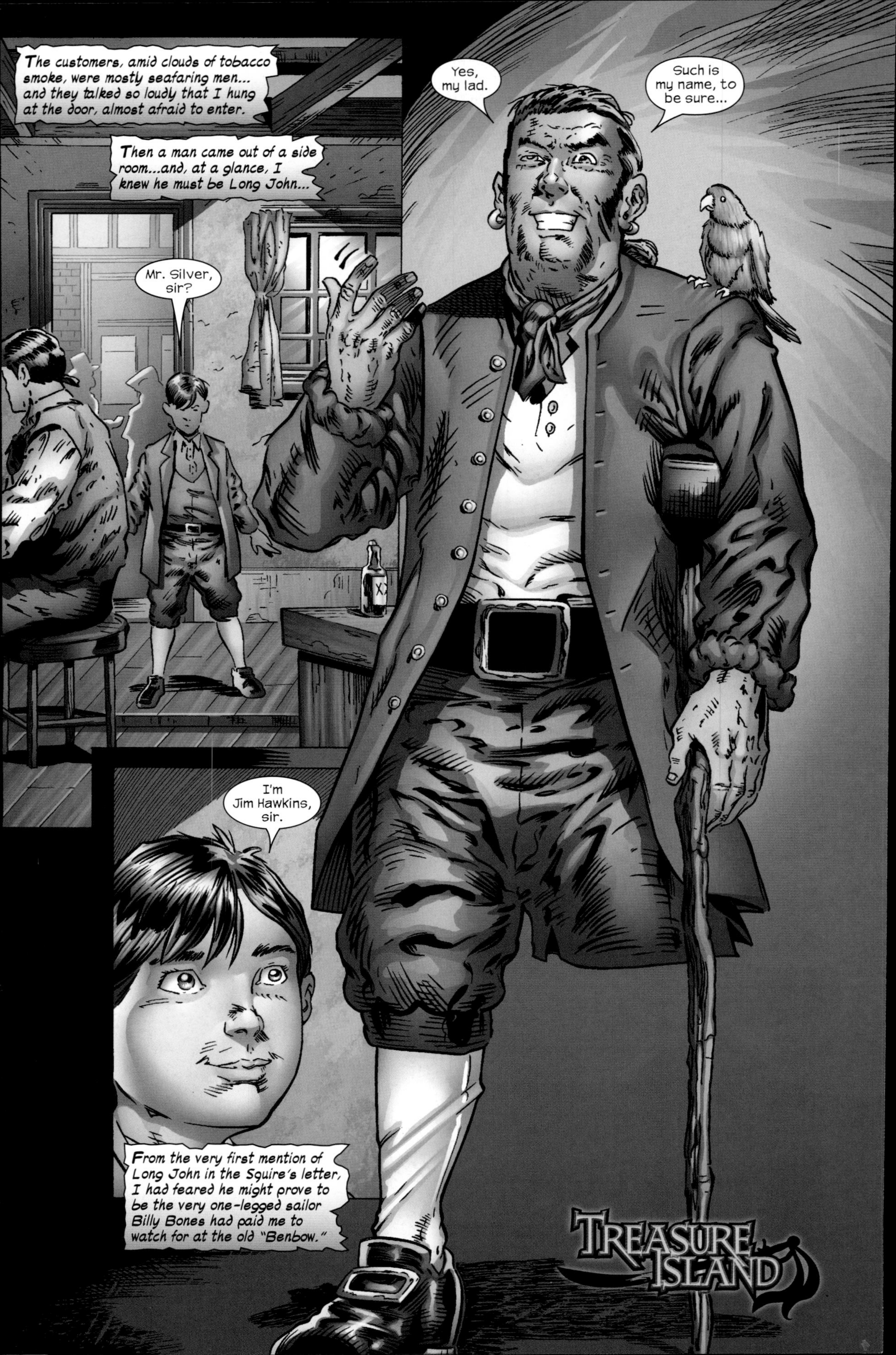

The customers, amid clouds of tobacco smoke, were mostly seafaring men... and they talked so loudly that I hung at the door, almost afraid to enter.
Then a man came out of a side room...and, at a glance, I knew he must be Long John...
Mr. Silver, sir?
Yes, my lad.
Such is my name, to be sure...
I'm Jim Hawkins, sir.
From the very first mention of Long John in the Squire's letter, I had feared he might prove to be the very one-legged sailor Billy Bones had paid me to watch for at the old "Benbow."
TREASURE ISLAND

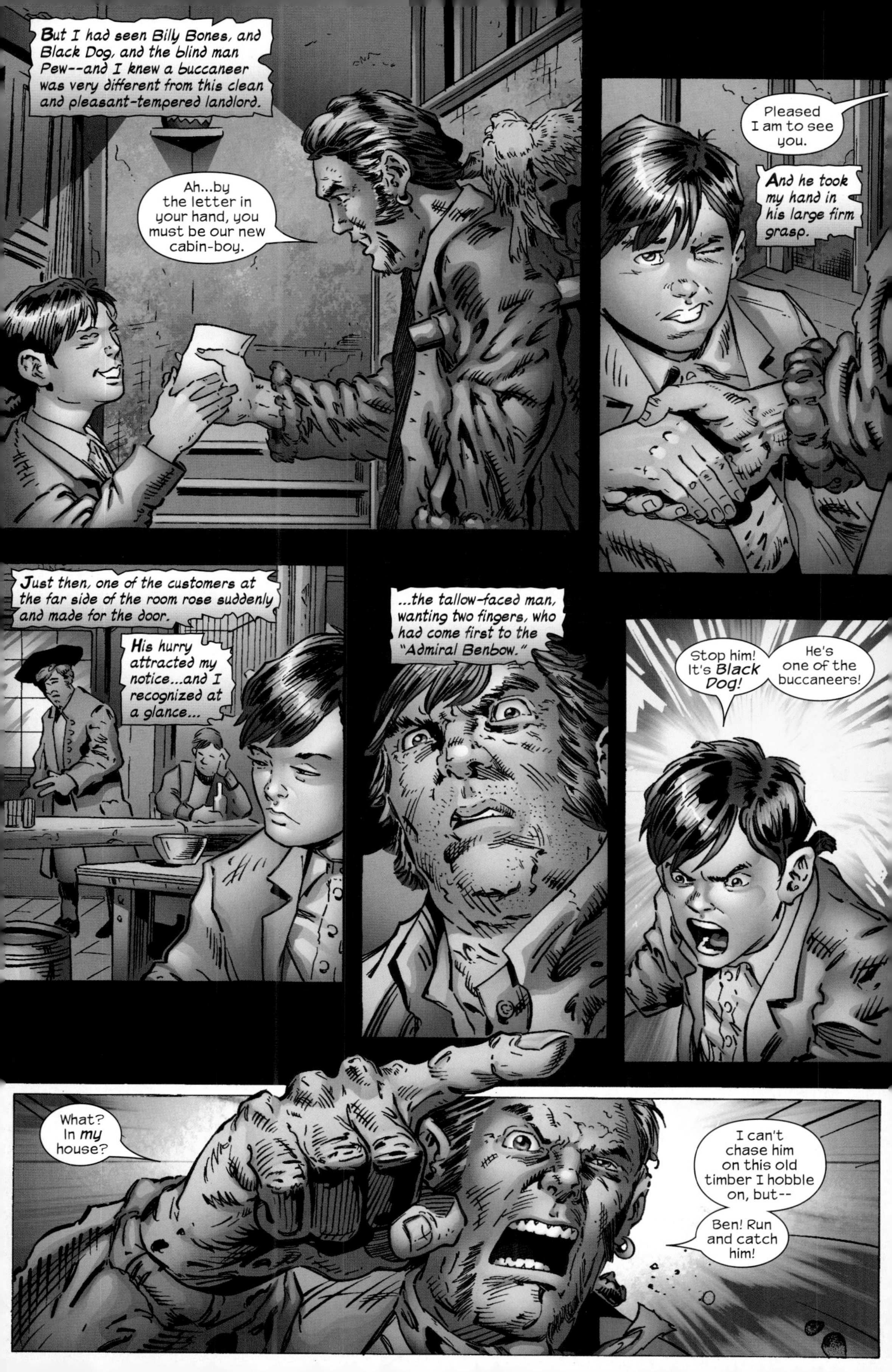
But I had seen Billy Bones, and Black Dog, and the blind man Pew--and I knew a buccaneer was very different from this clean and pleasant-tempered landlord.
Ah...by the letter in your hand, you must be our new cabin-boy.
Pleased I am to see you.
And he took my hand in his large firm grasp.
Just then, one of the customers at the far side of the room rose suddenly and made for the door.
His hurry attracted my notice...and I recognized at a glance...
...the tallow-faced man, wanting two fingers, who had come first to the "Admiral Benbow."
Stop him! It's Black Dog!
He's one of the buccaneers!
What? In my house?
I can't chase him on this old timber I hobble on, but--
Ben! Run and catch him!

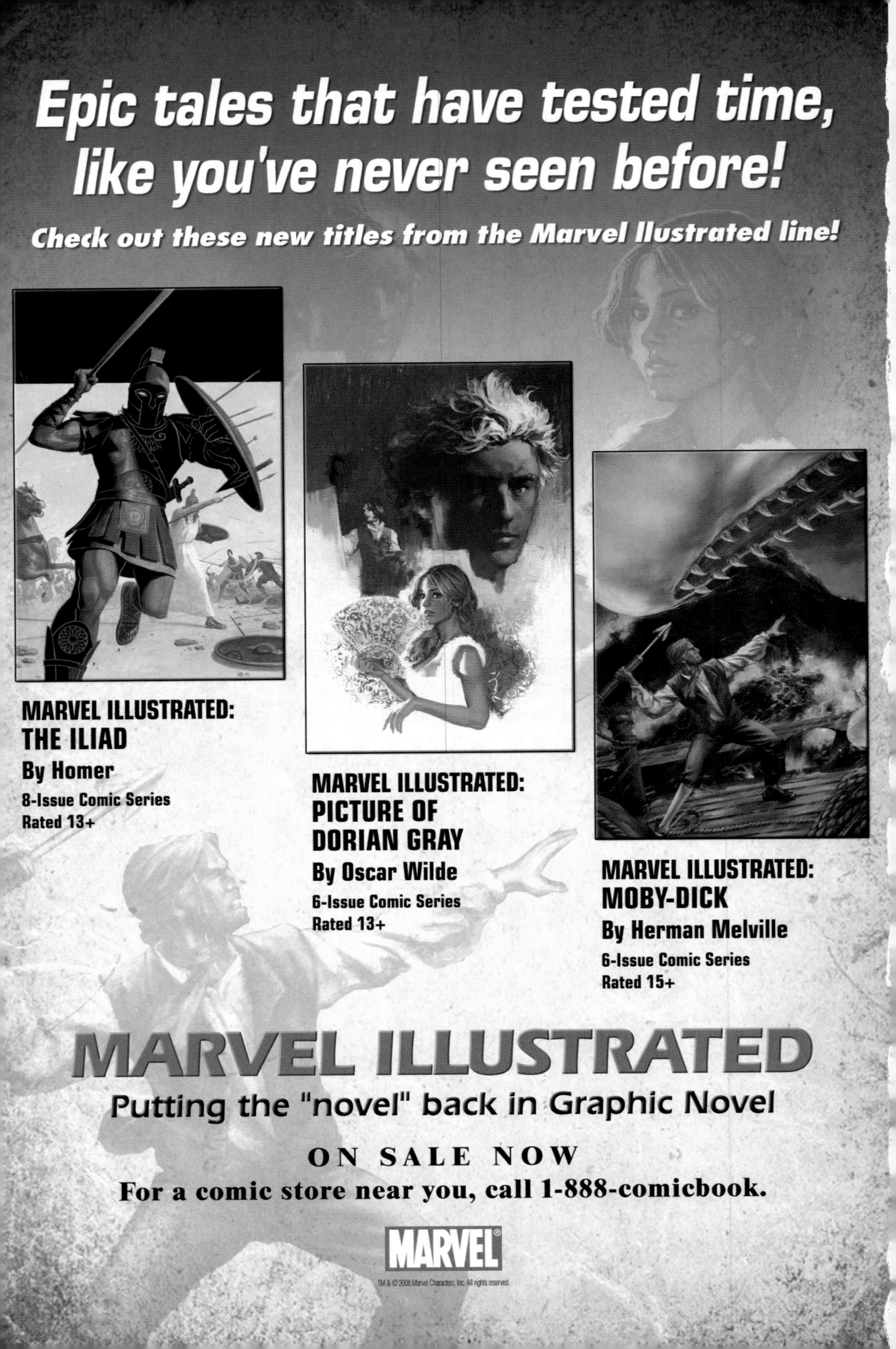
Epic tales that have tested time, like you've never seen before!
Check out these new titles from the Marvel Ilustrated line!
MARVEL ILLUSTRATED: THE ILIAD
By Homer
8-Issue Comic Series
Rated 13+
MARVEL ILLUSTRATED: PICTURE OF DORIAN GRAY
By Oscar Wilde
6-Issue Comic Series
Rated 13+
MARVEL ILLUSTRATED: MOBY-DICK
By Herman Melville
6-Issue Comic Series
Rated 15+
MARVEL ILLUSTRATED
Putting the "novel" back in Graphic Novel
ON SALE NOW
For a comic store near you, call 1-888-comicbook.
MARVEL
TM & © 2008 Marvel Characters, Inc. All rights reserved.